Healing From Childhood Trauma

How To Recover From Sexual, Physical And Emotional Abuse

By Phillip Newton Psych LPC

ABOUT THE AUTHOR

When you say that it is not easy to feel the shame and stigma associated with childhood abuse, I hear you. Being a victim myself, I was extremely unhappy with my life. However, I was lucky enough to find the right help regarding the trauma I faced during my childhood. Instead of hiding my pain, I used it for a better purpose. I pursued my career in rehabilitation so that I can help everyone out there who is living a life of misery even when they are not at fault. Being a rehabilitation specialist, I know how to tackle the issues related to childhood abuse. My clinical expertise and research-oriented knowledge make me an authority in this field. Above all, I was a victim myself, who has changed his life from negative to positive, and I am here to help you achieve the same.

Table of contents

ABOUT THE AUTHOR II

INTRODUCTION 1

CHAPTER 1: THE HEALING POWER OF COMPASSION AND SELF-COMPASSION 5

CHAPTER 2: HOW AND WHY CHILD ABUSE CREATES SHAME 10
    SHAME: THE MOST DESTRUCTIVE OF HUMAN EMOTIONS 12
        Distinguishing Shame from Guilt 12
    "VICTIM" OR "SURVIVOR"? 13
        Emma's Story: Debilitating Shame Caused by Emotional and Physical Abuse 14
    WHY IS IT SO DIFFICULT TO HEAL FROM THE SHAME? 16
        Internalized Shame 17

CHAPTER 3: WHY SHAME IS SO DEBILITATING 19
    THE MANY LAYERS OF SHAME 21
    SHAME IS NOT A SINGULAR EXPERIENCE 24
        Feelings of being humiliated 24
        Feelings of impotence 24
        Feelings of being exposed 25
        Feelings of being defective or inferior to others 25
        Feelings of alienation and isolation 25
        Feelings of self-blame 25

Exercise: Your Feeling Experience of Shame 26

Severe Effects of Shame 26

Moderate Effects of Shame 27

Exercise: How Debilitating Shame Has Affected You 28

DEFENDING AGAINST SHAME 28

Passive Strategies 28

Aggressive Strategies 29

CHAPTER 4: HOW COMPASSION CAN HEAL THE SHAME OF CHILDHOOD ABUSE 31

HOW COMPASSION CURES SHAME 32

Exercise: Becoming Compassionate Toward Yourself 33

THE BENEFITS OF PRACTICING SELF-COMPASSION 33

CHAPTER 5: TALKING ABOUT SELF-COMPASSION 35

THE OBSTACLES TO SELF-COMPASSION 36

THE FEAR OF DEVELOPING WEAKNESS, LAZINESS, OR SELFISHNESS
.... 38

The Belief That You should take the blame 39

A Refusal to Acknowledge Your Own Suffering 39

NOT UNDERSTANDING HOW YOU SUFFERED 41

Neglect 42

EMOTIONAL ABUSE 42

Psychological Maltreatment 42

Physical Abuse 43

Sexual Abuse 44

SUBTLE FORMS OF EMOTIONAL ABUSE 45
SUBTLE FORMS OF PHYSICAL ABUSE 46
SUBTLE FORMS OF CHILD SEXUAL ABUSE 46
YOUR REACTIONS TO THIS INFORMATION 47
    Releasing Your Anger 47
    Obstacles to accept compassion 48
    Living in a Culture of Denial and feeling undeserved 49
    Having Difficulty Taking In the Good 50
    Keeping Our Emotional Walls High 51
RECEIVING THE COMPASSION YOU MISSED OUT ON 51
    Taking In Words of Compassion 52

CHAPTER 6: FIVE WAYS OF RECOVERING FROM THE ABUSE 53

SELF-UNDERSTANDING 54

    Post-Traumatic Stress Disorder 56
    Complex Trauma 57
    Trauma-Sensitive and Trauma-Informed 58
CONNECTING BEHAVIOR AND EXPERIENCE 60

EATING DISORDERS 60

SELF-INJURIOUS BEHAVIOR 61

    Using Substances to Manage the Impact of Abuse 61
    Depression 61
    Anxiety 61
    Inner turmoil and pain 62
    The absence of all feelings 62
    Passivity 62

    Excessive anger and rage 63
An Opportunity For Self-Understanding 63
    Grounding 64
    Putting your behaviors in context 64
Repeating the Cycle of Abuse 65
Sam's Story: Repeating What Was Done to Him 67
    What Do You And Your Parents Have In Common? 69

CHAPTER 7: SELF-FORGIVENESS 72

The Obstacles to Self-Forgiveness 72
Forgiving Yourself for the Abuse Itself 73
    Abuser traits 73
    Abuser beliefs 74

CHAPTER 8: SELF-ACCEPTANCE 76

Your Critical Inner Voice 77
    How to Identify Your Inner Critic 77
    Your Inner Critic/Your Parents 78
    Noticing Your Critical Messages 79
Talking Back to Your Inner Critic 80
    Countering Your Inner Critic with Compassion 81
Creating a Nurturing Inner Voice 82
Set More Reasonable Expectations for Yourself 84
    It Is More Reasonable 85

CHAPTER 9: SELF-KINDNESS 86

    WHAT DOES KINDNESS FEEL LIKE? 86

        Words of Kindness 87

        Defining Self-Kindness 89

    A WORD OF WARNING 90

CHAPTER 10: SELF-ENCOURAGEMENT 93

    HOW TO PRACTICE SELF-ENCOURAGEMENT 93

    TALK TO YOUR INNER CRITIC IN A COMPASSIONATE WAY 94

        Compassion for Your Inner Critic 94

CHAPTER 11: HOPE 97

CHAPTER 12: CLARITY 100

CHAPTER 13: HEALING 106

CHAPTER 14: CHANGE 111

        Mindfulness 115

    MINDFULNESS PRACTICE 118

CHAPTER 15: GETTING CLEAR 124

        Taking Action 125

        Gratitude 126

CONCLUSION 127

RESOURCES 129

© **Copyright 2021 Philip Newton M. Psych LPC - All rights reserved.**

The content contained within this book may not be reproduced, duplicated or transmitted without direct written permission from the author or the publisher.

Under no circumstances will any blame or legal responsibility be held against the publisher, or author, for any damages, reparation, or monetary loss due to the information contained within this book. Either directly or indirectly. You are responsible for your own choices, actions, and results.

Legal Notice:

This book is copyright protected. This book is only for personal use. You cannot amend, distribute, sell, use, quote or paraphrase any part, or the content within this book, without the consent of the author or publisher.

Disclaimer Notice:

Please note the information contained within this document is for educational and entertainment purposes only. All effort has been executed to present accurate, up to date, and reliable, complete information. No warranties of any kind are declared or implied. Readers acknowledge that the author is not engaging in the rendering of legal, financial, medical or professional advice. The content within this book has been derived from various sources. Please consult a licensed professional before attempting any techniques outlined in this book.

By reading this document, the reader agrees that under no circumstances is the author responsible for any losses, direct or indirect, which are incurred as a result of the use of the information contained within this document, including, but not limited to, — errors, omissions, or inaccuracies.

INTRODUCTION

You must be familiar with the shame and stigma if you are a victim of childhood abuse or neglect. I know about this because I have been a victim, and trust me, it was not an easy task to escape the eternal misery. I am very glad that you have this book as your own savior. I overcame the problems and obstacles related to childhood trauma through the help of professionals and caregivers who worked very hard and helped me overcome the challenges. I promised myself that I would help millions of people who struggle with childhood abuse. I have studied and extensively researched the trauma associated with childhood abuse. As a victim myself, I have life-long experience and have helped many people struggling to find a way towards recovery.

You have likely been by the thoughts of childhood abuse for the better part of your life. You feel ashamed because you blame yourself for this. People who have been sexually abused tend to suffer most from shame. Those who have been emotionally, verbally, or physically abused tend to blame themselves. No matter how much you have been told that it's not your fault, you still blame yourself for it.

In case of emotional or physical abuse from a family member or caretaker, you may blame yourself for not listening to them. Children often blame the abuse or neglect they experience on themselves, and as an adult, you may have continued this rationalization. As an adult, you may put up with the poor treatment by others as you believe that it is all is your fault. On the contrary, if a good thing happens to you, you may become uncomfortable as you feel unworthy.

Former abuse victims are extremely ashamed and unable to express their anger towards the abuser; they may hurt or take the offense out on the weaker or their young siblings. This has been the case with many of my clients and myself. As they grow up, they tend to become bullies, and as they become adults, they resort to drugs or stealing to act against and show resentment towards society.

Don't worry, because I am here to help you through this. It is fine if you feel uncomfortable remembering the abuse. With scientifically proven strategies, you will learn how to become a more confident and resourceful person.

How Shame Affects Victims of Abuse
If you had been a victim of childhood abuse, shame could affect literally every aspect of your life. It can lower your self-esteem, self-confidence, and the way you perceive yourself. Shame alone is responsible for personal problems such as:

- Self-blaming or self-criticizing.
- Neglecting yourself.
- Showing self-destructive behaviors (taking drugs, harming yourself, or being accident-prone).
- Getting in fights and self-sabotaging behavior.

- Feeling unworthy of good things.
- Believing everyone is disgusted by you.
- Being critical about others.
- Experiencing intense rage.
- Going against society (stealing, breaking the law).
- Repeating the cycle of abuse.

Victims of childhood abuse experience a complete change in personality and the way they behave. This is mainly because these victims feel the loss of innocence and dignity, and they tend to carry a heavy burden of shame with them. These feelings overwhelm the victim so much that they stigmatize and hide from their true selves.

Shame is the center or core of every form of abuse. Guilt drives the cycle of abuse in various ways:

- Shame makes the victim believes that they are not worthy of being loved or respected. This causes them to stay in abusive relationships.
- Shame causes the victims to believe that they deserve disrespect and disdain from the hands of others.
- Shame can also cause the victim to have anger-related issues. They may humiliate or degrade their partner or children.
- Those who abuse are often trying to get rid of the shame they carry.
- Shame can cause a random outburst of anger and gives way to abusive behavior.

- Shame also causes the victims to resort to drugs.
- The victims tend to accept the unacceptable, and they readily accept the abusive behaviors of others.
- It can also cause the victims to become abusive towards people who they deem weak.

The good news is that you are not alone; tens of thousands of others are in the same boat as you. The even better news is that there is a method to heal and improve; all you have to do is change your view of the world, and I will assist you in doing so.

As I also suffered from these miseries, I have thoroughly researched this segment in my professional career and came up with the best explanation and solutions for childhood abuse. Every detail in this book is added after comprehensive research, and everything related to childhood trauma is addressed.

CHAPTER 1: THE HEALING POWER OF COMPASSION AND SELF-COMPASSION

For the better part of my adult life, I have been dealing with the victims of childhood abuse. I still continue to find more effective ways to help my clients. Many psychotherapists and advocates believe that shame is among the most long-lasting effects of abuse, and many victims have difficulty dealing with it.

After many years of research and study, various strategies can help in handling the shame. Like poison, toxic shame also needs to be countered with an antidote such as compassion, and being kind towards the victims is one way to deal with guilt.

Many researchers believe that compassion, kindness, support, and encouragement have a massive impact on our brains, bodies, and a general sense of well-being. Love and kindness affect how some of our traits and behavior develop.

One of the common findings in the research literature is that greater self-compassion is linked to less psychopathology. Studies revealed that showing compassion to yourself has a positive effect on depression, anxiety, and stress.

Self-compassion is also known to provide resilience as it moderates people's reactions towards adverse events, particularly trauma. Compassion helps in deactivating the threat system. It is found that individuals with higher self-compassion tend to cope better with upsetting events.

There is also evidence that self-compassion also helps people diagnosed with post-traumatic stress disorder (PTSD). Victims with higher self-compassion showed less severe symptoms. Shame is a significant component of many mental health problems and has been a critical factor in proneness to aggression.

Various key strategies and group therapies that work, particularly with shame, guilt, and self-blame, successfully reduce the depression, victim's tendency to self-harm or attack others, and feeling of inferiority. In addition, self-compassion is an antidote to self-criticism. Self-kindness, a significant component of self-compassion, allows human beings to see themselves as valuable beings worthy of love, care, and support.

In addition to offering compassion to the victims, I suggest that they regularly practice and learn self-compassion to get out of the ongoing struggle with shame.

Self-compassion is a proven technique and a result-oriented concept. It helps the victim to connect with their traumatic patterns. It allows them to communicate with the memories at a distance but not actually re-experience the abuse but remembering it to become their own compassionate witness. In this way, self-compassion helps the victim develop compassion for the child they once were without becoming the child. This technique is helpful as there is less chance that the victim will be re-traumatized, and it allows them to become the loving guardian they longed for. It gives them a path to heal themselves and learn how to treat themselves better, lovingly and kindly.

Part I of this book explains the link between childhood abuse and shame. This book provides a detailed description of the specific patterns of painful and harsh thoughts, feelings, and behaviors that victims of abuse find themselves in. Part II of this book examines the problems and obstacles that childhood abuse victims will face on their path to recovery. Part III of this book outlines various strategies to help abuse victims recover from struggling aspects of their lives.

One of the strategies that help abuse victims is compassion. Compassion has five components:

- Self-understanding.
- Self-forgiveness.
- Self-acceptance.
- Self-kindness.
- Self-encouragement.

It may take weeks or months to go through the entire rehabilitative process as it requires consistency and complete dedication. I highly recommend completing these exercises, which are specifically designed to help you benefit from each component. Some of you may want to read the entire book and then do the activities, and some of you may want to do the exercises while reading the book. It is entirely ok whichever regime you want to follow, do what you feel is easy and comfortable for you.

Since shame can lead you towards self-harming behavior and cause you to have suicidal thoughts, recklessness, and self-mutilation, you must seek professional help if you are experiencing any of the symptoms mentioned above.

SPECIAL BONUS!

Want this bonus book for free?

Get FREE unlimited access to it and all of my new books by joining the Fan Base!

SCAN W/YOUR CAMERA TO JOIN!

CHAPTER 2: HOW AND WHY CHILD ABUSE CREATES SHAME

If you are a victim of abuse in your childhood, chances are, you still suffer from the negative effects of this traumatic experience. These effects may include self-criticism, neglect, self-destruction, drug addiction, eating disorders, and perfectionism. The victims also tend to sabotage their relationships or career. You have also likely joined different programs and therapies to receive help, but the one problem you struggle to cope with is that debilitating shame. It is regarded by professionals as the biggest obstacle that adult victims of child abuse face.

I have had many clients who suffered from debilitating shame, and the guilt was so consuming that it was negatively affecting their different aspects of life.

Although everyone experiences shame from time to time, adult victims of child abuse have far more issues related to shame when compared to other people.

Shame is a natural reaction to abuse, as abuse is humiliating and dehumanizing by nature. This is a feeling of being helpless and at the mercy of another person.

These feelings are not only persistent in victims of sexual abuse but with victims of all abuse. For instance, physical abuse is not only an assault on the body but an attack on a person's integrity. Emotional abuse is also regarded as the murder of the soul.

Name-calling, constant criticism, belittling, and unreasonable expectations are different forms that cause emotional abuse, and they can be just as harmful as sexual or physical abuse. I firmly believe that emotional abuse's adverse effects last longer and have far-reaching consequences, and I am speaking all of this because I am an abuse victim myself.

Victims who were abused in childhood tend to feel shame as adult human beings. We want everyone to perceive that we are in control of our lives. When we are victimized, we feel humiliated. We regret and ponder that we should be in power, but because we cannot control the situation, we feel ashamed. It is very traumatizing and shameful for children when a parent abuses them. Physical abuse sends the message that the child is terrible and unlovable. Children simply want to be loved, appreciated, and accepted by their parents. As parental love is essential, children will do different things to grasp their attention. Most of the time, children blame themselves when they are abused at the hands of their parents.

Shame: The Most Destructive Of Human Emotions

If you ask anyone about the most destructive human behavior, most of them will choose anger or fear. But actually, it's a shame. Shame is the root cause and source of violence, cruelty, destructive relationships, and many addictions. It can damage the self-image and shatter the confidence and self-esteem to the point that the victim becomes self-destructive.

Shame is hard to identify and is more insidious as compared to other emotions. It takes over your mind and body. It makes you feel weakened, flattened, and deflated. Some people describe shame as a burning sensation, while others describe it as hot and numb. Many people say that they are unable to speak or think. Shame is a feeling of being exposed and unworthy. When we are ashamed, we want to hide and vanish. This shows from our actions; our head stoops low, and we curve our body inwards to become invisible.

Shame also makes us feel isolated and feel apart from other people. Being ashamed feels like being banished and unworthy to others.

Distinguishing Shame from Guilt

There is an informal agreement between therapists about the difference between shame and guilt. Although both are very similar, guilt can be understood as feeling disappointed in oneself for committing a specific behavior. While with shame, one can feel disappointed even though there was no violated behavior involved.

Some explained the difference between shame and guilt as when we feel guilt. We feel wrong about something we did or refused to do. When we feel shame, we feel wrong about who we are. In other words, guilty people fear punishment, and shame makes a person feel abandoned.

Another difference is that we don't tend to feel bad about feeling guilt. In fact, it is viewed as a positive thing, especially how others perceive you. If you feel guilty about something you did, there is a high chance that other people will forgive you. But shame is such a taboo topic that we feel shame about feeling shame, and this is all due to the strong correlation between shame and inferior feelings.

"Victim" Or "Survivor"?

Another thing that needs to be addressed is using the term 'victim' or 'survivor. It is more critical when we are describing an adult who was abused as a child. This argument is never-ending as a survivor because the word is more empowering than a victim. But the thing is, many clients I have dealt with said that they were offended at being called a survivor, especially when their victimization was recent and they were just starting to heal from abuse. They told me they would prefer the word survivor when they have had substantial recovery from the abuse. Being called a survivor also makes them feel as their victimization is being glossed over. Due to this feedback and working closely with the abused adults, I prefer to use victims as they are still in the recovery phase. It's not like I don't want you to feel empowered; it is just that I don't want to minimize the abuse that you have experienced by avoiding the term "victim."

I hope that my use of the word "victim" doesn't offend you. If you consider yourself a survivor, then feel free to substitute the word victim with survivor. I genuinely respect your choice, and from my personal experience with abuse as a child, I can genuinely relate to your preference.

In this book, I have also added cases of my clients that I've worked with over the years. (Names and identity details are changed to protect their confidentiality).

Emma's Story: Debilitating Shame Caused by Emotional and Physical Abuse

Emma came to me for help regarding her self-esteem.

she told me that she didn't feel good about herself, and she let people walk all over her. she said that she struggled to stand up for herself. as an adult, she told me that she couldn't control her children as they would get their way all the time.

when I inquired why she didn't feel good about herself, she told me she didn't like her appearance. she told me that she had a problem with her weight.

Like Emma, many people seek therapy as they have low self-esteem and are self-critical. They have difficulty standing up for themselves, even against those who are abusive and demanding. I later learned that her root problem was due to shame. It was causing all of the negative feelings.

Growing up, Emma's mother was very critical and demanding of her. Her mother would force her to do a task all over again if she wasn't pleased. She constantly yelled at Emma, and she would scold and criticize her for overeating. After learning about her, I wasn't surprised by Emma's problem. She had built a poor image of herself due to her mother's ill-treatment and constant body shaming.

An interesting fact was that Emma didn't consider her mother's ill-treatment as abuse. She would describe her as a "taskmaster" as they'd grown up in poverty. She scolded Emma to get good grades and made her do work all over again as she wanted her to have a good work ethic.

After several sessions, Emma opened up about the physical violence her mother would inflict on her. She would beat her for not doing the task correctly or for having average grades at school. One time, When Emma rebelled and snapped back at her mother, she told me that her mother's face turned bright red, and she leapt on her and beat her violently, which left her bruised.

When she opened up, she was not complaining about her mother. She just let me know what an obstinate child she was and blamed herself for her mother's abusive behavior.

If you are a victim of childhood abuse, there are high chances that your life has been plagued with debilitating shame, but like Emma, you may not have realized it yet.

Why Is It So Difficult to Heal From The Shame?

Those working closely with childhood abuse victims know how complicated the healing process is, which involves addressing and reducing clients' shame. It is difficult as the victim may realize that they didn't cause the shame, but they will still end up blaming themselves. For many victims, blaming themselves is easier as it is harder for them to imagine someone close to them, such as a grandparent, friend, aunt, or uncle, abusing them. Some victims may feel that they were enjoying themselves at some point during their victimization, which can explain why they might not have stopped it from happening. The same reason is with the victims of physical abuse; they feel that they deserve the beating at the hand of their parents or relatives. They think that being irresponsible in childhood is the reason that they got the beating.

Some parents believe that shaming their children will make them obedient and make them behave. Little do they know, this breaks their spirit, and they grow up either hating their parents or fearing them throughout their childhood.

This makes the victim rigid, close themselves up, and not let anything good come in.

this makes the healing process challenging as they require time and resources to feel safe and open up.

Internalized Shame

Internalized shame is a deep sense of who a person really is. Victims with internalized shame feel defective and unworthy. It becomes their foundation, and they start to feel that everything around them is inadequate and not good enough. The shame becomes so intense that it takes the shape of the victim's identity.

Internalization makes the victims feel shame on their own. They no longer need to be made ashamed to feel this condition. They only need a memory or a hint to trigger the shame. This causes victims to live in a constant state of self-blame and self-criticism.

They find it impossible to take compliments, love, and admiration from others. Some of the shame-bound people also resort to depression and anxiety. These people are, in a true sense, broken by debilitating shame.

Some of the people suffering from shame chose anger as a defense mechanism. They attack others before they have a chance to attack themselves. This approach drives people away, even if they are just trying to help them.

Carrying debilitating shame is like constantly being weighed down by a heavy burden. The shame continues to fester like an open wound that doesn't heal.

CHAPTER 3: WHY SHAME IS SO DEBILITATING

Shame is a sickness of the soul.

Terry is a sex addict. Unlike ordinary men, he thinks about sex all day. He told me that he had lost his wife and kids and ruined his career in a session. He has lost his self-respect due to his addiction. His addiction has put him in highly hazardous situations, especially when he is having illicit sex. He said that he is lucky that he hasn't got AIDS or been killed in an alley.

Kelly also suffers from alcohol addiction. Before she came to me for help, she had been in rehabilitation facilities for four years. During her last stay in the rehabilitation center, she realized that she was numbing her childhood abuse memories through alcohol. She said that she wanted to deal with her abuse as she kept relapsing due to nightmares.

John came to me because he had problems maintaining good relationships. He said that it wasn't long before he started to push away people close to him, even if they were good. He would say or do something so insulting to them that they wouldn't come near him again. He wanted to know what was wrong with him and was struggling to figure out a solution.

Thomas has been in sessions with me for quite some time. He came to therapy after he realized that his wife emotionally abused him. Ironically, his wife thought she was being used in the relationship when she read the book 'Emotionally abusive relationship.' She gave the book to Thomas, and when he read it, he realized that he was the one being abused. He couldn't believe how he could let his wife degrade and humiliate him.

While the problems with the people mentioned above are different, the common thing they all have is that they all suffer from debilitating shame. They are so overwhelmed that they behave in self-defeating and self-destructive ways.

Terry was sexually abused by his grandfather when he was five, and it continued until he was ten. The circumstances around the abuse haunt him every day. He said that he hated everything about himself. Terry noted that abuse brought pain and disruption in familial relationships. He told me that when his grandmother saw his grandfather sexually abusing him one day, she was so disgusted that she threw his grandfather out of the house; afterward, she couldn't look Terry in the eyes. The family adored my grandfather and blamed me for what happened to him as they couldn't see him even on holidays.

There was no one to tell Terry that the sexual abuse wasn't his fault. He wasn't responsible for the divorce of his grandparents. He was not responsible for his grandfather's banishment and his dying in a little apartment all alone. The shame that Terry had to endure was so overwhelming that his daily acts were now driven by shame. This also caused him to always think about sex, and he introduced his neighborhood kids and little cousins to sex.

Kelly was also sexually abused in her childhood, but instead of being driven by the shame, she started to numb the memories by consuming alcohol.

John pushed people away because he thought that he was not worthy of good things in life. He had been emotionally abused by his father, overtly and deliberately. It seemed that John's father was hell-bent on destroying his son's confidence.

Thomas being abused in his wife's hands further added to the shame he already felt because his parents verbally and physically abused him as a child. He was so emotionally distraught that he had little motivation left to make his life better.

These clients represent examples of how shame creates distress and havoc in victims' lives.

The Many Layers of Shame

Being victimized is a shaming experience. It brings humiliation as you feel violated and feel that you have no control over your life.

Projection can also be a significant aspect of shaming. Most abusers are projecting their own shame by abusing their victims. In many cases, it is the abuser's motivation, however unconscious. Many of my clients admitted that their abusers had already been abused in their past.

When the abuse is exposed, it furthers adds to the shame. This is apparent in the case of Terry.

In Terry's case, his grandmother's reaction was shaming. With her comments and attitude, it seemed that all of what had happened was Terry's fault. She treated him as if he had enticed his grandfather into molesting him. The reaction of the family was also very disgusting towards him. They openly spoke about how the grandfather lived all alone and how much they missed him. Instead of helping Terry heal, they further added to his shame.

Many of the victims are shamed by the reaction of those to whom they open up to. One of the primary reasons for this is that nobody believes them. This was certainly the case with me. When I opened up to my mother about being molested, she didn't believe me. She said I was doing this to get attention. This added to the shame and humiliation that I was already feeling due to the molestation.

Some parents or relatives shame the child by saying that he has falsely accused the perpetrator, making the child believe that he was somehow the offender. In Terry's case, all family members rallied around him and asked how he could lie and blame such a sweet old man who had always been good to him.

Victims also feel shame when they have to describe the whole scenario to the police or authority. If the victim ends up in court, it further adds to the shame of publicly speaking about it. Conversely, some clients reported that it felt good when they opened up, and many victims feel good when they make an outcry.

Finally, there is a shame that victims have to endure in coping with the abuse. We can see in the examples how Terry began to re-enact his own abuse with other children. We can see in Kelly's case when she became an alcoholic and failed three stints in rehab. In John's case, he was ashamed as he had hurt so many people in his life who had been good to him. Thomas had to suffer from the emotional abuse at the hands of his wife.

It's essential to realize that there are many layers of shame due to childhood abuse:

· The shame that comes from being violated and feeling helpless and hopeless.
· The shame children feel when their parents are disappointed in them.
· The shame victims take when they project their shame on others.
· The shame that comes from being unable to cope with the previous burden of guilt.

When we see how many layers of shame add up, we understand that it can be challenging to heal, and the healing process will take its time and course. The healing process will need time, patience, and understanding.

Shame Is Not a Singular Experience

Indeed, shame due to abuse in childhood is not from a single source; it's also true that it is not a singular experience. It is a cluster of different experiences and feelings. This can include:

Feelings of being humiliated

Abuse is very humiliating for a victim, but some types of abuse are much more humiliating than others. For instance, sexual abuse always has an extra element of humiliation. As it violates the human body and a child knows incest is taboo, an additional embarrassment is profound, especially if it gets public exposure.

Feelings of impotence

When a child realizes that they are powerless and helpless to stop the abuse, they feel unsafe all the time, even long after the abuse has stopped.

Feelings of being exposed

Abuse and the feelings of vulnerability and helplessness make the child feel self-conscious and exposed. The fact that they couldn't stop the abuse makes them feel weak and exposed even in their adulthood.

Feelings of being defective or inferior to others

Most victims describe their feelings as damaged, defective, used, and corrupted following the abuse.

Feelings of alienation and isolation

The trauma follows the feelings of being different, less than others, or cast out. Although abuse victims may want to talk to someone about their suffering, they feel immobilized, trapped, and alone.

Feelings of self-blame

Victims of abuse blame themselves for the suffering and for feeling ashamed. This is the case when the abuse starts happening in childhood.

The following exercise will help you discover the primary feelings of shame.

Exercise: Your Feeling Experience of Shame

Although you may have experienced the feelings mentioned above, you may resonate with some more than others. Think about each type of abuse and the feelings associated with it. Ask yourself which of the elements below stand out. These are the primary feelings of your shame.

The Effects of Shame

The nature and severity of shame can depend on these factors:

- The relation with the person who is inflicting abuse.
- Public shaming or private shaming.
- The number of times the abuse is happening.
- Presence of emotional support during abuse.
- The capacity of the victim to cope with the abuse.

The abuse at a stranger's hand may be less shaming for the victim than the abuse from close relatives. The same is the case in that scolding a child publicly in front of their peers can be more shaming for them if it was done privately.

I particularly find it helpful to divide the effects of shame into two categories: severe and moderate.

Severe Effects of Shame

These effects include:

- Feelings of self-hatred, self-sabotaging, and self-loathing, which can lead to self-destructiveness.
- Self-destructiveness may include thoughts of self-harm and self-mutilation
- Self-neglect includes not providing enough for oneself for the body's good survival.
- Re-enacting the abuse you endured. This can make the former victims become abusers. This can also make the victims allow others to take advantage of them repeatedly.
- Drug addiction or alcohol addiction to numb the suffering and pain and addiction can also include gambling, sex, and pornography.
- Victims can be bitter, hostile, and abusive towards others.
- Victims can remain isolated for long periods.

Moderate Effects of Shame

These effects include:
- Sensitivity to positive criticism and correction in which victims' shame can be easily triggered.
- Creating a defensive wall between oneself and others.
- Victims can be self-critical, harsh, and unforgiving of themselves.
- Perfectionism to avoid further shaming.
- Inability to speak up for themselves.
- People-pleasing behavior to avoid further shaming and abuse.

- Lack of motivation and being confused around tasks.
- High expectations from themselves and others.

Exercise: How Debilitating Shame Has Affected You

- Take a look at the severe and moderate effects of shame, notice which of them apply to you. (You may experience effects on both lists).
- Don't get worried or overwhelmed if you realize what extent of abuse you are suffering and how it has affected your life at this point. Just go slow with the pace.

Defending Against Shame

Every person feels shame when they feel they are being exposed and humiliated. Typically, people feel shame for some time and allow it to pass on. But abuse victims tend to internalize shame. Their personality and day-to-day activities start to drive from shame.
Some of the strategies used against shame are:

Passive Strategies

Examples of defensive strategies in which the person turns the shame inward include:

- **Internal withdrawal:** The person withdraws deeper inside to escape the pain that comes with exposure and rejection. They engage in fantasies to gain positive feelings.
- They are escaping from the problems and isolating themselves. Victims tend to keep their distance from others and lock themselves in places they believe are secure.
- Victims try to be pleasing to others and become overly submissive and non-assertive. They put the needs of others over their own.
- Victims try to follow perfectionism to avoid shame by never making mistakes again.
- Blaming oneself when something goes wrong
- Continually comparing oneself to others and feeling inferior (A classic example of low self-esteem)

Aggressive Strategies

Examples of defensive strategies in which the person copes by turning shame outward include:

- Becoming aggressive and belligerent is a self-protective strategy.
- Being judgemental, critical, or condescending towards other people around.
- Strive for power and control to compensate for defectiveness that surrounds the internalized shame.

- Making someone else feel ashamed reduces your own guilt.
- Victims tend to identify with the aggressor. They take their qualities and start to defend them.

All of the strategies mentioned are temporary fixes. These strategies will temporarily alleviate the feelings of pain, shame, and suffering. None of these strategies actually address the root cause.

The following exercise will help you consciously identify the type of defense you took on against shame.

Exercise: Which Defensive Strategies Did You Take On?

Go back over the strategies above and see which one applies to you. There can be several strategies that you may have taken. Don't be surprised if the strategy is a mixture of passive and aggressive.

One thing to note is that don't criticize the strategy you may have taken in the past. Just remember that the path you took was just to take care of yourself and protect yourself.

CHAPTER 4: HOW COMPASSION CAN HEAL THE SHAME OF CHILDHOOD ABUSE

Compassion is the radicalism of our time.

— The Dalai Lama

My new client Harvey hated to talk about his childhood. He said that talking about his childhood made him depressed. He told me that his father mistreated him and that his father used to make him feel small and inadequate. Harvey said that he used to walk around with his head down, and he felt like he didn't deserve to be around other people.

I asked why he chose to come for therapy. Harvey said that no matter how hard he tries, he can't get rid of the image of his father standing over him and telling him how terrible he is. Harvey told me that he feels good about himself, but when the images of his father appear, all of the good gets wiped away.

I have explained earlier how abuse victims tend to feel powerless and helpless and how quickly these feelings turn to shame and humiliation. Many victims like Martin believe that becoming powerful and gaining power over others will heal the shame, and they thereafter no longer feel helpless and powerless.

As I have a long experience with clients suffering from childhood abuse and personal experiences with abuse, I have concluded that compassion is a great tool that can cure shame and end the suffering of victims when used in the right way.

How Compassion Cures Shame

Compassion helps to soothe the hurting feelings, and it comforts the pain. It neutralizes shame. When someone shows compassion, they're offering a healing elixir.

When somebody joins us in the suffering, they provide us with not one but five healing gifts:

1. They let us know that they are aware of our distress. The victim's fundamental need to be seen is one of their most basic demands. This is especially true for those who have been abused as children.
2. They let us know that they hear us.
3. They let us know that it is ok and we have the right to express our pain, sadness, fear, and anger.
4. They let us know that they care about us as human beings, and they recognize our suffering.
5. They offer us comfort and soothing in some way and help us to heal from the suffering.

Exercise: Becoming Compassionate Toward Yourself

1. Consider the most compassionate person you've ever met—someone who was kind, empathetic, and encouraging towards you. A teacher, a friend, a friend's father, or a family who might have been involved. Consider how this individual expressed their concern for you and how you felt in their presence. Take note of the emotions and sensations that this recollection generates. Consider a sympathetic public person or even a fictional character from a book, film, or television show if you can't think of someone in your life who has been compassionate to you.

2. Now imagine being as sympathetic to yourself as this person has been to you. If you would overcome with sadness or guilt, how would you treat yourself? What would you say to yourself if you were talking to yourself?

The Benefits of Practicing Self-Compassion

Learning self-compassion will help you in the following way:

- It will help you to acknowledge your pain/suffering honestly and will help you to heal.
- It will help you to take in compassion from others.
- It will help you to reconnect with yourself and your emotions.

- It will give you closure and an understanding of why you acted out negatively.
- It will help you to stop blaming yourself for victimization.
- You will be able to forgive yourself for the ways you tried to cope with the abuse.
- You will learn to be kind towards yourself.
- It will help you to reconnect with others and become less isolated.

CHAPTER 5: TALKING ABOUT SELF-COMPASSION

It is not easy for people to practice self-compassion who have suffered from abuse in their childhood. It is also not easy for them to accept compassion from someone else. There are many reasons for this. First, most of the victims were not raised with compassion. Secondly, most people with a history of childhood abuse haven't practiced self-compassion and were never told to be self-compassionate. Third, there are many obstacles and resistance for victims to accept the concept of self-compassion.

You don't suddenly become self-compassionate; it's both a process and a practice. It will take time to practice self-compassion daily. There is no need to push yourself if you are not feeling ready. I'll lay the groundwork for compassion by introducing different ways of thinking.

I'll also teach you mindfulness techniques that will aid you in coping with the feelings that will eventually come up as you continue to face the truth about your abuse. By the time you have completed this part, you will be willing and will be able to begin self-compassion practice, which is later discussed in section 3 of the book.

The Obstacles to Self-Compassion

It is understood that those who were abused in their childhood have trouble practicing self-compassion as many haven't been treated with compassion when growing up. In this chapter, we will discuss the obstacles that victims have to face when practicing self-compassion. I will also help you fully understand how you were abused and how it has affected you.

Self-Compassion Is Self-Indulgent-A Wrong Belief

The most prevalent impediment to learning and practicing self-compassion is that many victims regard self-kindness, which is an important component of self-compassion, as a self-indulgent quality. This belief is especially harmful when taken on by victims of abuse and neglect, who need self-compassion to heal. Culture discourages people from acknowledging and talking about their sufferings. It's considered a sign of weakness. Victims are supposed to "get up and move on."

Expectations of instant recovery are very unnatural and unreasonable. It takes time to recover from the abuse, and the healing process takes its course. The healing process requires the victim to acknowledge their suffering and adversity.

People who show self-denial about their suffering will find that pretending to move on will eventually catch up in the form of health issues, many of which are related to stress. These people also become intolerant of others' pain and sufferings. They think that other people should get over it as they did as a victim of abuse themselves.

Acknowledging your suffering with self-compassion is not whining, self-pity, or feeling sorry for yourself. When experiencing self-pity, we complain about the dire situation and see ourselves as helpless people who can't change it. There are often bitter thoughts and feelings associated with these feelings.

Self-compassion comes from a nurturing place that is inside us and is comforting and validating. Here is the difference between self-pity and self-compassion described by my client Rose:

Self-pity: "no one likes me, and I don't have any close friends. I'm going to end up alone in my life."

Self-compassion: "it's a sad state in which I am in now. I don't have any friends or a man in my life. I'm afraid that I will not have friends or a man in my life ever due to my history, and it's understandable why I have this fear."

Rose then told me that self-pity left her bitter and made her hopeless. But after she started practicing self-compassion, she told me that acknowledging that she felt sad and afraid eventually made her feel better. And using the phrase, "it's understandable," validated her experience. She told me that being self-compassionate kept her motivated and really helped in improving her situation.

The Fear Of Developing Weakness, Laziness, Or Selfishness

Some individuals worry that being kind to themselves would make them weak, and they will lack the motivation to survive in tough situations. But when we look at history and look at personalities famous for their compassion, such as Jesus, Buddha, Mother Teresa, and Nelson Mandela, their work and struggle can hardly be regarded as weak or unsuccessful. Being self-compassionate actually makes one stronger and confident.

One client told me that it was good for him whenever he got hard on himself. He said that he was used to getting lazy and complacent otherwise. It is worth noticing that being hard on yourself doesn't really pay off and is not beneficial in the long run. It is far more productive to acknowledge the difficulties and appreciate yourself on how far you have come. Encouraging yourself increases your drive to become more successful.

Some people think that being self-compassionate is a selfish trait. As a child, we are taught to put the needs of others ahead of ours. It is for the betterment of society. Because of this misbelief, some people may consider self-compassion as a selfish characteristic.

The Belief That You should take the blame

As discussed earlier, believing that you are the reason for your own abuse gives you some sense of control. However, this is a false belief as it is taking you away from the reality that the abuse was not your fault and that it was just an unfortunate event that took place. This event shouldn't have happened in the first place.

Since shame is so debilitating, human beings would do anything to try to avoid it. Having a sense of control makes us feel safe, and we are raised believing that we are responsible for anything happening to us. Thus, when something wrong happens, we tend to feel ashamed.

There is also a victim-blaming mentality in our society. In addition, some have spiritual beliefs that something wrong happens to you due to negative energies. Cultural influences like this segregate and blame the victims.

A Refusal to Acknowledge Your Own Suffering

We can't get going if we don't acknowledge our pain. Denial serves as a powerful and effective defense mechanism. In some instances, we wouldn't be able to exist without denial. Some children, for example, have been badly mistreated to the point of suicide. If children allow themselves to acknowledge the abuse they are taking from the hands of their abuser, they may not be able to stay sane. Denial can be your friend, and, at times, it keeps you sane in unbearable situations. But it is important to know that you will not fully heal until you face the actual truth about your abuse.

Some victims often make excuses for their abusers; they do this to minimize the damage. Sometimes they straight out deny their abuse. They need help to take such blinders off and allow their suffering to surface. The following exercise can help in this regard.

Exercise: Your Childhood from a Different Perspective

I want you to write your childhood story and write from the perspective of someone else. Be a storyteller (there was once a little girl who had a stepfather). The child in the story is the subject. Give details about what happened to the child. Please keep the perspective of the storyteller who knows what happened to the child.

This exercise will help you to view your childhood from a different perspective. It has helped many of my clients.

_____
_____
_____
_____

Not Understanding How You Suffered

Another reason many of the victims resist acknowledging their abuse is that they simply don't understand how they have suffered from their torturous experiences. Either they are unaware of how the abuser has abused them, or they are unaware of how abuse itself has affected them.

This section will describe various types of emotional, sexual, and physical abuse endured by children. I really believe that his section will assist you in two possible ways:

1. It will remove the denial about the fact that you were indeed abused.
2. It will help you identify how you were abused (also the ways of abuse you were not aware of).

Many victims try to clear the memories of abuse or neglect as children. But for some people, these memories are unclear. Some of the questions are still attached to these traumatic experiences. I've given a brief overview here about what is considered childhood abuse and neglect. All of these can occur separately or in combination.

Note: Some of the below-mentioned acts of abuse can be disturbing.

Neglect

Neglect of a child happens when a caretaker or parents fail to provide basic needs for the child. This includes food, water, shelter, and attention that they need growing up. Please keep in mind that failure to meet these demands only applies in this case if caretakers are eligible to meet the basic needs of their families.

Emotional Abuse

The child's emotional abuse includes acts or omissions by parents or caretakers that cause serious behavioral, emotional, mental, or cognitive disorders. Verbal abuse, placing excessive and unreasonable demands on the child, and failure to provide emotional and psychological support are different forms of maltreatment in emotional abuse.

Psychological Maltreatment

Emotional abuse is sometimes considered a type of psychological ill-treatment. Professionals use this term to describe a concentrated attack by an adult on a child's self-competence and social expertise. This treatment is often deliberate on the caretaker's or parents' part. This maltreatment is classified into the following forms of behavior:

- Behavior that communicates abandonment of the child.
- Prevention of the child in participating in everyday activities.
- Threatening the child with severe punishment.

- Being emotionally and psychologically unavailable to the child.
- Encouraging the development of misleading societal values that promote corrupt behavior in the child.
- `Deliberately withholding love, affections, support, and guidance.
- Acts or behavior that humiliates or degrades the child.
- Refusal to provide for the activities and experiences that child needs for proper growth and education.
- Exposing the child to unhealthy and destructive role models.
- Forcing children to live in dangerous places and unstable environments.

Physical Abuse

Any non-accidental physical harm or pattern of injuries to a child (under the age of eighteen) is considered physical abuse. This might involve the following:

- Slapping or punching a child so hard that it causes bruising.
- Kicking a child with so much force that it knocks them down and causes injuries.
- Beating a child with a hard object.
- Burning them with cigarettes, hot spoons, or putting their hand in a fire.
- Biting a child.

- Twisting a child's arms or legs to the point where it fractures or bruises.
- Shoving a child's head underwater.
- Pinning a child to the floor.
- Hitting a child's head in the wall.
- Pinching a child with so much force that it causes unbearable pain and can lead to bruising

Sexual Abuse

Any interaction between an adult and a child, or an older child and a junior one, for the purpose of sexual stimulation, is considered sexual abuse. This abuse can range from non-touching offenses, such as exhibitionism or showing pornography, penetration, creating child pornography, child prostitution, or fondling.

It is assumed that an older child is two or more years older than the younger child, but even a minimal age difference can also have tremendous implications.

Child sexual abuse can include the following:

- Exposure of genital area.
- Kissing intimately.
- Fondling with the child's body parts.
- Masturbating in front of a child.

- The child is forcefully convinced to put his mouth and tongue in the genital area, or the adult laces their mouth in the child's genital area.
- Thrusting of inanimate objects into the vagina or the anus of the child.
- Penetrating genital area with penis.
- Showing pornographic material to the child.

Subtle Forms of Emotional Abuse

Emotional abuse can take many forms, including:

- Ignoring or withholding affection, love, or attention from the child.
- Being disapproving and dismissive of the child's behavior and giving them the silent treatment.
- Giving subtle threats of abandonment.
- Not acknowledging the child's feelings or experience.
- Making a child feel unwanted.
- Projecting one's own problems and issues on the child.
- Causing a child to feel inadequate or incapable

Sometimes parents try to shame their child into behaving, but they don't know the disruptive impact on the child's sense of self.

Parent also shame their child by telling them that they are such a disappointment. Parents used to tell their children that they would never be good enough. Telling the child that your parents are very disappointed in you crushes the child's spirit. These messages are a form of exceeding expectations.

Subtle Forms of Physical Abuse

Although emotional abuse typically includes non-physical forms of abuse, it can also include symbolic abuse. This violence includes intimidating behavior such as throwing dishes, slamming doors, kicking a wall, or generally destroying things around.

Subtle physical abuse also includes keeping a strap, belt, or paddle on display all the time, so the child is intimidated. This is also done to make a child behave in a certain way, and when the child doesn't do what the parents want, they point them towards the belt or strap.

Subtle Forms of Child Sexual Abuse

A subtle form of sexual abuse includes:

- Nudity.
- Disrobing in front of a child.
- Observing the child when they bathe or undress.
- Passing inappropriate comments that are sexual in nature in front of a child.
- Touching a child in a sexualized way.

- Being seductive and intimate with a child or sharing intimate sexual details with the child.
- Making a direct or indirect sexual suggestion towards a child.

Your Reactions to This Information

While reading this section, you may have had strong reactions, such as surprise, shame, or anger. You may be shocked at the degree of denial that you were going through. However, you must have compassion for yourself instead of criticizing yourself for something that you didn't have any control over.

You may be overwhelmed with anger or disbelief about how much abuse you have sustained throughout your childhood. It is common for victims to feel a great deal of anger and rage due to their victimization. You have every right to be angry, and it is a natural reaction. Releasing this anger can motivate and empower you. The good news is that there are ways through which you can safely release your anger. I have discussed these below.

Releasing Your Anger

Some healthy and constructive ways to release your anger are:

- Write a letter to your abuser and let them know how you were affected. Let all your feelings and anger come out on-page.

- Walk around the house assuming you are alone and talking loudly to yourself, express all the rage and anger you are having.
- Imagine your abuser sitting in front of you. Tell them everything without censoring anything, and don't hold back. And if you are afraid of the abuser, assume they are tied to a chair.
- Put your face into a pillow and scream.
- If you need to release your anger physically, find a safe and satisfying way to do so. For example, hitting the mattress of your bed is a safe and satisfying way to release the rage.

Receiving Compassion from Others

In the previous section, we discussed the obstacles in practicing self-compassion. In this section, we will focus on how to overcome these common obstacles.

Obstacles to accept compassion

Many victims refuse to take compassion from others as they believe they don't deserve it and don't need it. For instance, when I try to be compassionate with my clients, they start to downplay it by saying abuse hasn't affected them that much in their lives and say that they have gotten over their abuse.

If you somehow relate to these types of statements that my clients express, chances are that you are still in some form of denial. The following exercise that I have included can help you look at the denial and better understand why it is such a strong force.

Exercise: the exploration of your denial

1. Because _____, it is hard for me to acknowledge that I was mistreated in this way.
2. Admitting that I was abused will make me _____
3. If I confess the extent to which the abuse has damaged me_____
4. I don't want to confront my abuser while knowing the painful truth because it will_____
5. Because _____, I'm hesitant to let myself experience my anger or despair.

Living in a Culture of Denial and feeling undeserved

Our culture typically frowns upon those people who acknowledge their sufferings. In fact, our culture has a habit of celebrating people who overcame or moved on from their woes. People want to face everyone with a happy face and don't want others to start talking about their problems. It is so common for people to put on a happy face, yet if someone gives them news about their sufferings, it comes as a shock to them. Many people who were abused in their childhood are so ashamed that they believe they don't deserve compassion from others. You should feel no shame in reaching out to those who can provide the compassion that you need.

Having Difficulty Taking In the Good

Another primary reason victims feel that they don't deserve compassion is that they have difficulty accepting anything good. You start to push away people who are good to you simply because you believe you aren't worthy of these good things and behavior. Victims have a hard time accepting gifts or compliments from others.

Many of my clients tell me that they put the gifts in a drawer or a closet and don't use or see them; they usually give them to someone else. Some say that they get critical and start complaining about the gifts. Some victims even avoid acknowledging the thought of having gifts or compliments.

Taking a compliment and gifts can easily make you uncomfortable when you are not feeling good about yourself and believe that you don't deserve good things. The same goes for compassion if someone else is giving it to you. So, the next time you receive a gift or a compliment, try the exercise I've added below.

Exercise: Learning to Take a Compliment

1. Don't say anything right away and hastily.
2. Take a deep and relaxed breath and imagine taking the compliment.

3. Notice how it feels. If it makes you uncomfortable, try to allow it by not being judgmental.
4. Breathe out and say thank you to the person. Try to add something positive, and if not, give a neutral response. If you have an urge to say something negative, try to resist it. Try to have a genuine smile when saying thank you.
5. Take some time and reflect on the exercise. Try to write up any feelings or memories that came up during this exercise.

You can also do the same exercise when you receive a gift. When taking a deep breath, take some time to imagine how much thought and time this person gave while choosing this gift.

Keeping Our Emotional Walls High

The reason some people have difficulty in taking compassion from others is that they feel vulnerable. If you have built up a wall to shield yourself from shame, it may become difficult to lower it to let compassion in. Some people become so overwhelmed with grief and pain that they start to disassociate from it. Others feel that it will be soon taken away from them if they allow kindness and joy.

Receiving the Compassion You Missed Out On

Now I will offer you a safe environment, kindness, and support that you may not have received while growing up.

Taking In Words of Compassion

Imagine you are sitting with me in any environment you are comfortable in. Take the list you made earlier about how in different ways, you were abused as a child. Slowly read that list in silence and notice how you feel. Reread this list this time loudly. Now imagine me saying these words to you:

"I'm sorry for all of the things that happened to you. I'm sorry you were abused in these ways. I want you to know that I understand your sufferings. I know you have felt alone, and no one could possibly understand how you are feeling. I understand all of this because I have been an abuse victim myself and have survived all of these horrific feelings. Many clients have told me their stories, and it has given me a deep understanding of how abuse can make people suffer. No one should go through this torment. I believe that knowing someone cares for you makes suffering a little more bearable."

Sit back quietly and try to take in my words. Reread the words again and take deep breaths until you can take the words in.

CHAPTER 6: FIVE WAYS OF RECOVERING FROM THE ABUSE

There is a proven strategy that helps with practicing compassion. This strategy has five components which are:

1. self-understanding.
2. self-forgiveness.
3. self-kindness.
4. self-encouragement.
5. self-acceptance.

This strategy is designed to teach victims of child abuse about the following attitudes and skills.

- How to view your symptoms and negative ways of coping.
- How to forgive yourself for the harm you have caused to yourself or others.
- How to understand the negative power of self-criticism and focus on yourself.
- How to have inner strength and warmth against self-attacking thoughts.
- How to substitute self-criticism with self-kindness.
- How to have compassionate feelings for yourself, and how to soothe yourself in positive ways.

- How to know about your strengths and work on them.
- How to appreciate yourself.
- How to practice accountability instead of criticizing yourself.

The amount of shame the victims of child abuse go through makes it impossible for them to practice self-kindness unless or until they decrease the amount of shame they carry. This is because these victims believe that they don't deserve self-kindness.

To practice self-kindness, victims need to practice three components: self-understanding, self-acceptance, and self-forgiveness.

Self-Understanding

It is one of the essential components of the strategy we are studying. By gaining self-understanding, you will relieve yourself of the burden and shame you are carrying due to abuse. Without self-understanding, it will be nearly impossible for you to practice the other four components.

Like many victims, you may be overwhelmed by the shame of being abused and that shame you have to carry due to self-harming behavior. This shame can interfere with your ability to be self-compassionate. Self-understanding can be the key that will help you open the doors of self-compassion. Victims tend to continue harming themselves without self-understanding and letting themselves feel down for their mistakes and shortcomings.

Victims who were abused in their childhood are very hard on themselves. They set high expectations for themselves and to achieve them. They make many mistakes that further cause them to have no mercy on themselves and have no excuse policy for their behavior. This situation is unfortunate as you don't allow yourself to acknowledge the pain and sufferings, and you expect yourself to walk away from abuse unscathed.

The fortunate thing is that you may be aware of how trauma has affected you. For comparison, let's say you were in a plane crash, and you survived it. Your physical injuries are now healed. But the events during the impact you had to go through are traumatic. The realization that your life was in danger and the fear of what would happen was horrible. The terror of pain, overwhelming sights, and sounds are itself very traumatic. Even though you survived, you still have to take this trauma with you. You will replay the crash over and over. You will experience nightmares for quite some time.

The same is the case of child abuse victims. In addition to the shame, they have to carry the trauma and stress of these memories. And, this stress and trauma take their toll on the victim. I have often found myself explaining to clients that I have actually never met a victim of childhood abuse who didn't react to the abuse with problematic behaviors—abusing alcohol or drugs, acting out, sexual or other addictions, self-harm, abusive behavior toward loved ones, or a pattern of staying in abusive relationships.

Throughout this chapter, I aim to encourage you to connect with your past and current behavior and the traumatic experiences. This will help you to be compassionate with yourself.

Post-Traumatic Stress Disorder

PTSD or post-traumatic stress disorder is a severe anxiety disorder that develops after extremely traumatic events. This can be severe injury or being in life-threatening situations. This can also be from the violent assault that damages personal pride and integrity.

People diagnosed with PTSD have nightmares and flashbacks of the traumatic events. They have difficulty sleeping, and they feel detached and estranged. To make matters worse, PTSD often occurs with related disorders such as substance abuse, depression, and the problem of memory and cognition. In some cases of PTSD, symptoms become more debilitating than trauma.

PTSD further impairs the person's ability to function socially and in family life, including troubled marital life, family discord, difficulty in parenting, and occupational difficulties. Those people who are diagnosed with PTSD are vulnerable to repeating cycle of violence due to the following reasons:

1. Many people diagnosed with PTSD turn to drugs and alcohol to get relief from their symptoms.

2. Some people may develop abusive behavior and may have trouble controlling their anger.
3. Some victims may develop victim-like behavior. They may indulge in self-blame, feel helpless, and have a sense of being tainted or evil.

Complex Trauma

Children who have suffered from multiple chronic traumas suffer from unusual setoff symptoms that can differ from the symptoms of PTSD. These children tend to suffer from serious interpersonal, functional, and behavioral problems. This is known as complex trauma.

This particular group has high rates of depression, drug and substance abuse, personality disorders, and anxiety/stress disorders. Unless victims don't overcome these adverse effects of trauma, they may continue to experience this throughout their lives.

Victims of complex trauma tend to experience:

· Extreme behaviors such as self-injury, cutting, and headbanging.
· Sexual acting out.
· Getting into high-risk and painful situations.
· Sudden and repeated outbursts of anger.
· Extreme behaviors (self-injurious behaviors such as cutting, headbanging).

· Severe sexual acting out (addictions to illicit sex or pornography; reenacting sexual trauma).
· Creating high-risk or painful situations to counteract feeling numb or dead inside (self-harming behaviors).
· Sudden outbursts of anger.
· Suicidal ideation or suicide attempts.
· Extreme risk-taking behavior
· Reenacting unhealthy relationships

Trauma-Sensitive and Trauma-Informed

The expressions trauma-sensitive and trauma-informed allude to more supportive, caring, and compassionate ways of seeing the behaviors of victims who have been damaged and traumatized. The trauma-sensitive methodology challenges how we look and perceive trauma victims, helping and empowering them to treat themselves (and be treated by experts) with greater poise, regard, and sympathy than they normally do. The term trauma-informed suggests that victims and helpers are both trained in the consequences of trauma.

By treating yourself in trauma-sensitive and trauma-informed ways, you can easily increase your ability to be more compassionate. This helps you to be more empathic and empowers you to deal with your symptoms.

These are some of the principles of the trauma-informed way of thinking below:

- Trauma restricts the victim's choice and disturbs life. It undermines self-esteem and creates a sense of hopelessness and helplessness.
- Behavioral problems are adaptive responses to trauma. They should be viewed as an attempt to cope with past trauma.
- Substance use may have evolved as a coping strategy when options were limited.
- The focus should be on what happened to the victims rather than what was wrong with them.
- Victims are doing the best of their capacity to cope with the life-altering and life-shattering effects of trauma.

Instead of blaming yourself for the efforts you are putting in to manage your traumatic reactions, you can start to recognize the adaptive function of your symptoms. For example, you are consuming alcohol and other drugs to cope with the anxiety. You can begin to recognize this and have compassion for yourself. This is a significant change and step forward.

The benefits of trauma-informed thinking include:

- It helps you transform from being bad to being hurt. This opens a door for a more empathetic and constructive attitude towards yourself.
- It helps in externalizing your problems. You can view yourself as good with some issues that have intruded in your life, but they don't represent your true self.

- Trauma-informed helps victims show normal and reasonable reactions to the traumatic and unfortunate events.
- It empathizes the resources and strengths. As victims are very self-critical, they must look for their strengths and give themselves due credit.
- It helps victims to look for healthy and productive strategies to cope with trauma.

Connecting Behavior and Experience

Making the right connection between your behavior and trauma will help you be more compassionate and less judgmental, critical, impatient, and angry at your behavior. Some of the problematic behaviors are listed below. The list is not comprehensive, but it will help you understand the connection between troubled behaviors and abuse.

- Eating disorders.
- Self-injurious behavior.
- Drug abuse and substance use.
- Emotional dysregulation.

Eating disorders

Eating disorders include eating problems such as binging, overeating, and emotional eating because you were emotionally abused. These issues arise to cope with loneliness, depression, emptiness, or other forms of stress and anxiety.

Self-injurious behavior

This includes behavior like cutting or self-inflicted wounds, burns, or headbanging. These are attempts made to cope with severe abuse or abuse caused by multiple perpetrators.

Using Substances to Manage the Impact of Abuse

A person who has been abused emotionally, physically, and sexually has to suffer from powerful emotions and interpersonal chaos. Some victims believe and discover that they can get relief from pain by using drugs and alcohol.

Depression

Many of the victims report that they feel hopeless about their life. Using drugs like cocaine helps elevate the mood for a short time for the victims who experience depression for an extended period.

Anxiety

Victims of trauma feel anxious and fearful all the time. Alcohol and tranquilizers lessen the anxiety for the short term for the victims who constantly feel on edge.

Inner turmoil and pain

Victims who experience nightmares and flashbacks of the traumatic events may feel that the intensity of their experience is far too great. They might seek drugs that help them to forget and tend to dull or numb sensations. These victims are at high risk of choosing opiates or alcohol to reduce the pain.

The absence of all feelings

While some victims feel too much, some have reported that they are unable to feel anything. They said that they are unable to feel any sensations, from sexuality to happiness or sadness. Any substances that heighten the sensations are appealing to these victims. They may be drawn towards cocaine or amphetamines for adrenaline rush-type sensations.

Passivity

The long-term consequence of abuse is the Lack or absence of any motivation in abuse victims. These victims are unable to stand up for themselves. They report that they see no choice but to submit to someone instead of standing up for themselves. They wish that they could feel anger or assertiveness. Drugs such as PCP or alcohol appeals to these victims.

Excessive anger and rage

When victims accept what was done to them at the hands of the abuser, they may have overwhelming feelings of rage and anger. If they don't have access to the abuser, they may feel angry and find no outlet for their rage. In many cases, they turn to drugs and alcohol to feel less angry.

An Opportunity For Self-Understanding

You are more prone to use drugs to cope with traumatic symptoms if you often use drugs or alcohol for recreational purposes.

Try these sentence stems for the symptoms. This is an effective way and will be beneficial in the long term:

- Given my past associated with sexual abuse, it's normal that I'd try to drown out the pain somehow.
- Given my experience of abuse, it's understandable that I began drinking at such a young age.
- Given my history of abuse, it's understandable that I'd drink excessively.
- It's reasonable that I'd have a hard time quitting drinking given my abused childhood.

I recommend that you repeat the identical phrase stem as many times as necessary.

I suggest you use the same sentence stems, completing the sentence as many times as you can think of responses.

Grounding

Grounding is a powerful but simple and effective strategy to manage and relieve emotional pain, such as panic episodes, trauma flashbacks, and dissociating. Grounding is powerful because it can be used in any situation where you are caught in emotional pain. It can be done at any time and at any place.

It is important to note that grounding is not a relaxation technique. It is a tool often used for centering victims. Some of the victims with PTSD tend to become anxious when guided through conventional methods because hearing words like "relax" may be a trigger that can remind them of sexual abuse.

Most victims report that they feel more present after practicing grounding. Practice grounding whenever you are feeling extremely anxious.

Putting your behaviors in context

The following exercise will help you in building a better self-understanding:

Exercise: The Connection Between the Abuse and Your Behaviors.

1. Make a list of behaviors that causes you trouble. You can also write down what things you have done that caused the most shame.
2. Take a close look at the list and see if you can find the connection between it and your abuse experience.
3. Once you have the connection and know it is understandable, check whether you feel more compassion for yourself.
4. Next time, see if you are behaving in a self-destructive way. Instead of blaming yourself, try to say to yourself, 'I understand why I'm acting this way.'

Repeating the Cycle of Abuse

We have already discussed why abuse victims' resort to coping mechanisms like substance abuse, self-harm, sexual abuse, and other dangerous addictions. This section will focus on another reason why abuse victims tend to carry such a tremendous amount of shame.

This is a sad fact that no one gets through the abusive childhood experience unscathed. In many cases, those who were abused tend to become abusers as they grow up. Research reveals that those who experience abuse tend to absorb it and pass it on. Studies show that children who are abused and assaulted are at greater risk of becoming abusive towards their children when they become parents. Females who have been abused in childhood have a high chance of continued victimization even when they grow up.

A sexually abused male will be likely to harm his children sexually. If he marries a woman who was sexually abused, there is a high chance that she will become a silent partner. She will stand silently while her husband continuously molests their children.

Battered women are often and frequently misunderstood even by those who are closest to them. In my experience of dealing with many victims, there is always a good reason, and it only has something to do with an abusive childhood.

1. Make a list of all the reasons you cannot leave the situation or end the relationship (like a fear of being alone or not supporting your children, or believing that your partner will commit suicide if you leave them).

2. Now go back over your upbringing to see if there are any parallels to the above-mentioned reasons. You may have documented fear of being alone because you were frequently left home alone as a child with no one to look after you. You may possibly show worry about not being able to look after your children since your father abandoned the family and you went through a period where you didn't have enough to eat. The fear that your spouse may commit suicide may stem from your father threatening or committing suicide when your mother left him.

It is difficult for many of us, including the victims, to understand why a battered woman stays in an abusive relationship. It is even harder to understand why someone would abuse another human in such a brutal way.

Sam's Story: Repeating What Was Done to Him

Sam was my client in the early part of my career. He was required by law to seek counseling for abusing his wife physically. I was an intern, and at that time, I didn't completely understand why victims were used in this way. At that particular time, victims were thought to have anger management issues. Working with Sam was a gift because he gave me a deep understanding of the batter's plight.

Sam was initially defensive to the point where he argued and seemed utterly closed to any help I was offering. He was convinced that he was beating his wife because she wasn't listening to him, and the only solution to the problem in his mind was for her to do everything he asked her to do. While he realized that he had to stop beating her to avoid jail, he still didn't grasp the real understanding of why he shouldn't treat his wife like this.

After many sessions, I realized that Sam's behavior was a great deal of shame he was trying to suppress underneath all of this. It took a while, but I discovered that Sam's father was severely emotionally abusive towards him in his childhood. His father always undermined him and told him he was worthless and will not achieve anything in his life.

When I talked about this with Sam and how his father treated him, he tried to brush it off and said it wasn't a big deal and it was for his own good.

I was determined to help Sam, and I wanted Sam to be compassionate towards himself. I told him that his father didn't have any right to talk to him in this way. I told him that it was a bad situation that he had to go through. I politely told him that it was very mean of his father to attack his character.

At first, Sam argued and told me that he needed it when he wasn't good enough and said it made him strong. He told me that his father was trying to make him more responsible.

Over the next few months, Sam began to see the emotional abuse he had to endure from his father. He felt ashamed and humiliated. I continued to offer him compassion, and eventually, Sam started to realize that perhaps his father was way too hard on him.

The next stage was to help and encourage Sam to have compassion for himself. He began to recognize that he had been, after all, just a little boy and that his father's expectations were too high. He was able to get to the point to tell me that he didn't feel like a screw-up for the first time in his life.

By gaining self-understanding and connecting with his own suffering, Sam could have true and honest compassion for his wife's abuse. By the time Sam left the program, I was no longer worried about him abusing his wife again—but of course, I couldn't be sure. About six months later, Sam sent me this letter:

> I just want to tell you how much I appreciate the work you did with me. No one in my life has ever understood me the way you did. And no one has been so kind. You helped me to feel that maybe I could be kind to myself. I learned so much from you. Mostly, I realized that I didn't want to treat my wife and kids the way I was treated.
>
> P.S. My wife wants me to thank you too.

If you have become an abuser or abusive to anyone close, I hope the story of Sam will aid you in remembering that there is always a reason someone becomes an abuser. In fact, I have never known an abuser who wasn't abused in any way. However, it's just an explanation, not an excuse.

The following solution will help you see clearly how your current behavior represents your parents' or abusers' behavior.

What Do You And Your Parents Have In Common?

For this, you will need three or four pieces of paper.

1. On one piece of paper, write how your parents neglected you or were abusive towards you. This includes attitudes or verbal abuse.
2. On the second paper, write down ways other adults or your relatives abused you.
3. On another paper, write the ways you were neglectful or abusive towards your children. This list does not need to be read by anybody else. Making this list will be no doubt very painful, and you may try to lie to yourself. To break your shame while writing, take deep breaths and write again. Remember you are doing this to get better.
4. Compare the lists you made. Note the similarities in how you have been abusive or neglectful towards your children, partner, or others.

The Lesser-Known Consequences of Abuse and Neglect

There are also other subtle legacies of abuse and neglect. For instance, those with a history of abuse can often clearly see their children, partners, close relatives, or coworkers. They see them through the lens of fear, anger, distrust, and pain. They see signs of abandonment, betrayal, and rejection even though it's not there. Those who have been subject to abuse and neglect in the past are often unable to trust their partners. They also have issues with anger management. They also have high expectations from their children and don't want to see them make any mistakes.

Practicing self-understanding

Although some people are more resilient than others, the damage they have faced from abuse has long-term consequences. In this dilemma, gaining self-understanding will help you. It will stop you from adding more shame to your overwhelmed condition, and it will also act as a fuel to motivate you to change, grow and get better. It will also help you to stop being self-judgemental.

CHAPTER 7: SELF-FORGIVENESS

Everything you have read till now leads you towards this chapter. Self-forgiveness is a step you can take to eliminate debilitating shame.

Self-forgiveness is recommended only for those who are working to heal from abuse after-effects. It will help you in being more receptive to others. You will be able to recognize how you have harmed yourself. Your relationship with yourself will vastly improve.

Self-forgiveness is a healing medicine. It acts as a neutralizer towards the poison you get from shame. It soothes the body, mind, and soul. Self-forgiveness also facilitates the overall healing process.

The Obstacles to Self-Forgiveness

Just as there are obstacles in practicing self-compassion, there are also barriers in the way of self-forgiveness. You may view self-forgiveness as a tool to let yourself off the hook.

Another obstacle is that you may need to forgive your abuser. It is essential to forgive your abuser for self-forgiveness because after forgiving your abuser, you will be able to forgive yourself.

Another reason you might struggle with self-forgiveness is that you want to be nice and want to be in an ideal position. To be as good as you want yourself to be, you may become unforgiving of yourself because you have raised the bar to a level too high.

The final obstacle is the question that arises in many victims' minds. How does forgiving help those who have been harmed?

Forgiving Yourself for the Abuse Itself

Self-forgiveness always starts and ends with the abuse itself. I hope that what you've read this far will help you to stop blaming yourself. However, some people just refuse to accept that they are not to be blamed for the abuse they have endured, no matter how many times they are counseled about this. They are convinced that they are somehow responsible for the abuse they have suffered. This is highly likely for those who have suffered abuse at the hands of their parents.

Abuser traits

Those who have become abusive have certain predictable traits.

Those who are abusive have:

- Childhood history that involves emotional, physical, or sexual abuse.

- They tend to blame others for their problems.
- They have a strong desire to remain in control and a constant fear of things spinning out of control.
- They have difficulty empathizing with others.
- Inability to respect personal boundaries.
- Uncontrollable temper and anger.
- Being unreasonable and having poor impulsive control.
- They are emotionally needy and very demanding.
- Anger which is repressed.
- They suffer from stress and anxiety.
- They have an intense fear of abandonment and reflection.
- Narcissistic and selfish.
- They have poor coping skills.

Abuser beliefs

Those who are abused have certain beliefs about themselves. These beliefs set the tone of their relationship with others, and they can be abusive.

These beliefs include:

- The abuser is always right no matter what.
- It is always someone else's fault.
- Their need is of higher priority than others.

- They have a right to demand from others, and if they refuse, they are the enemy.
- They are better and superior to others.
- Other people's feelings are not important.
- Those who complain are too sensitive.
- No one should be trusted.

This person has an abusive personality if they often have the above-mentioned thoughts. Such individuals are abusive in most of their relationships, especially when they have authority and power right under their sleeves.

Knowing about the abusive personality and how this personality looks can help you understand that there is one person for abusing a child. It is never the child's fault.

I'm saying all of this because it is not your fault that you were abused. No matter the circumstances, it is always the fault of the abuser. I hope that it will give you clarity and a clear picture. There is absolutely nothing an innocent child can do to warrant abuse.

CHAPTER 8: SELF-ACCEPTANCE

Gaining self-acceptance can also be a natural outcome of self-forgiveness and self-understanding. When you behave as you wish and have forgiven yourself, you are more than likely to accept yourself for who you are.

Unfortunately, you will probably find it impossible for former abuse victims to see themselves in this way. Although forgiving yourself for your past mistakes may have helped you, if you continue to be self-critical and unforgiving of your ongoing mistakes, you will find out that you are accumulating your shame. While there may be many things that you want to change for yourself, you must develop self-acceptance. As abused children are often deprived of life and affection and are constantly called out for their mistakes, they must work towards self-acceptance and give themselves what they really deserve.

In this chapter, I will help you to change your lifetime shaming behavior through self-acceptance. It may not be easy to change it, but you can do it.

I encourage you to do the following:

- Try to discontinue behaviors that add to your shame. This includes being self-critical and overly judgemental.

- Understand that we all have weaknesses, flaws, and shortcomings, and recognize that they are all part of human nature.
- Confront your beliefs that you shouldn't make any mistakes, and you should always be perfect.
- Try to work on accepting yourself and keep in mind that you are prone to making mistakes. Try to forgive yourself for your past mistakes and also your current mistakes.

Your Critical Inner Voice

One of the significant steps towards developing self-acceptance is to turn off your inner critical voice. Instead, try to have a nurturing or compassionate self. Everyone has a critical inner voice but abusing this voice drives people crazy as it completely overwhelms them.

When a child is being abused constantly, he cannot keep these critical messages out. If the critical voice of the parent becomes your inner voice, it is then referred to as an introjected parent.

How to Identify Your Inner Critic

It can sometimes be challenging to identify your inner critic. This voice can seem natural and a normal part. But with every attack that this voice makes on you, it weakens you and tears you down slowly.

Your inner critic has many roles. It is detrimental because:

- It sets impossible and unachievable goals of perfection.
- It makes you guilt-ridden for small mistakes.
- It blames you for anything that goes wrong.
- It calls you derogatory names.
- It constantly compares you to others.

The following practice will help you reduce the negative messages that you have received from your parents.

Your Inner Critic/Your Parents

1. Write about what your parents wished for you and what you wished for them. What did they want you to do, and why did they want you to do it? How did they convey this to you, and how did it impact you?
2. Examine if your inner critic or judge behaves in the same way as your parents do. Do you relate to yourself in the same manner you interact with others?

The Pathological Inner Critic

Your pathological inner voice drives you to achieve unattainable standards. It keeps egging you to be your perfect image. It never leaves you satisfied and makes you feel incompetent.

Answer the following to see how powerful your inner critic voice is:
- Do you have high standards set for yourself?

- Do you spend significant time evaluating your performance?
- Do you feel okay after making mistakes?
- Do you feel regret for a long time after making a mistake?
- Is your mind constantly plagued with critical messages about yourself?
- Do you envy others and their success?

If your answer is yes to two or more questions above, your life is being dominated by your inner critic voice.

Noticing Your Critical Messages

1. Start by observing how frequently you receive critical signals in your thoughts. Keep note of how often you hear from your inner critic by maintaining a diary or writing it down.

2. Pay attention to when these messages appear, such as when you try something new or when someone compliments you.

3. It's also a good idea to jot down the content of any vital messages you receive. This will assist you in determining whose voice you will be hearing (perhaps your mother, your father, or another caretaker). The words and tone will most certainly bring back memories of how one or more of these persons spoke to you as a child (or even today).

Talking Back to Your Inner Critic

Although it is difficult to stop your judgmental and critical inner voice, you don't have to listen to it and be encouraged by it.

This inner voice is activated whenever you are feeling vulnerable and exposed. Once it is set in motion, it's a shaming spiral that gets more powerful. Therefore, you must externalize this inner dialogue to take away its power.

One way to counter is to talk back to it. You have to take it literally. We need to act decisively and right at the moment. This is done the same way you would put down a bully trying to hold you down. You cannot allow your inner critic voice to wear you down and slowly take you over.

Most people are afraid to talk back because some have their parent's voice as the inner critic. It may feel that they are talking back to them. If this idea scares you, take it slowly; talk back only when you feel brave and confident.

The following phrases have been particularly powerful in eliminating and silencing the inner critic's voice. Choose voices with which you are comfortable and confident, as well as statements that empower you.

- "I'm not buying it!"

- "This is dangerous. Put a stop to it!"
- "Get off my back!"
- "Waste of time!"
- "These are fabrications."
- "My mother told me the same falsehoods."

Countering Your Inner Critic with Compassion

Once you know more about your inner critic, you can utilize self-compassion to counter it. As compassion is an antidote to shame, it also acts as a neutralizer for your inner critic. When you are compassionate with yourself, you silence your inner critic.

Learning to be compassionate with yourself will also help you to realize your self-worth. It allows you to understand yourself better. You'll have no trouble forgiving yourself when you don't hear your inner critic criticizing you. When you hear your inner critic talking to you, respond with something like this:

- "I'm just doing the best I can."
- "I'm only human, and humans make errors,"
- "Given my circumstances, this is the best I can do right now."
- "I'm perfectly fine the way I am."

Creating a Nurturing Inner Voice

1) Sit in a comfortable position and close your eyes. As you conduct this technique, take a few deep breaths and establish a relaxing breathing pattern.

2) Place your right hand on your heart and hold it there. Feel as if all of your attention and awareness is directed there.

3) Visualize your heart opening up like a flower as you breathe in and out. Feel the brightness and love flooding your heart. Allow this love to begin the process of mending your heart from past hurts. Feel as this love is expanding and is spreading throughout your body. If you feel distracted by your thoughts, gently push them aside and focus on your heart.

4) Visualize the love radiating from your heart and extending throughout your entire body. Allow light and love to flood your body. If you find yourself being diverted by thoughts, gently push them away and return your attention to your heart.

5) Begin to cultivate a supportive inner voice. This isn't a harsh, judgmental tone, nor is it an unduly sweet, indulgent tone. It's a soothing, friendly, or any other

voice that makes you feel at ease. This voice will eventually become your own, but for now, it may be any voice you want: someone who has been nice to you or a favorite character from a film. If you're religious or spiritual, it may be what you picture God's, Jesus', or Buddha's voice would sound like.

6) If you don't hear any loving words, don't get upset. Some people have a more difficult time imagining and connecting with a kind, loving part of themselves than others. If this is true for you, here are some examples of kind words you can repeat to yourself while continuing to focus on filling your heart with love and light:

- I must accept myself in my original form.
- I should be gentler and more understanding about myself.
- I should give myself the compassion I need.
- I am lovable.
- I am confident.

Gently repeat the phrases you received from your caring inner voice or the keywords I've supplied while taking deep breaths. Continue to fill your heart with love and light. While doing so, gently touch your arm or hair, or hold your face in your hands.

When you're ready, gradually bring your awareness back into your body.

Repeat this process as many times as you can over the following several weeks. It won't happen overnight, but with practice, you'll be able to replace your critical inner voice with a more loving inner voice. This, in turn, will assist you in altering your self-perception and relationship with yourself.

Set More Reasonable Expectations for Yourself

You may have adopted this unjust and punitive attitude toward yourself due to the abuse you received as a child, which includes your parents having high expectations of you and punishing you when you were not perfect. You may create excessive objectives and expectations for yourself. You may always want to accomplish things right and without making mistakes. When you do make an unavoidable mistake or transgress, you are likely to be severe with yourself, chastising yourself as brutally as your parents did. You might be punishing yourself by starving yourself, depriving yourself of all nice things, or even harming yourself.

If you don't have reasonable expectations of yourself—expectations that are neither too harsh nor too lenient—you will constantly feel disappointed in yourself. It can activate your critical inner voice, and you will not take action to reach your true potential.

When examining the history of abuse, a fair expectation can be reached. Because of your abusive background, it's understandable that you would have poor self-esteem, a harsh inner critic, and pathological shame. Given your background, it's unrealistic for yourself to overcome the harmful consequences of abuse overnight. However, it is realistic to assume that by reading this book and working through the exercises, you will be able to begin to undo most of the harm you have endured.

Use the following exercise to understand some of your unreasonable expectations about your behavior and replace them with more reasonable ones.

Exercise: It Is More Reasonable

1. Think of any behavior that you would like to change. For instance, you want to improve your parenting skills.
2. This format is to be used so you can identify unreasonable expectations.
3. Given_____, it is illogical for me to_____

It is more logical for me to_____

Example: "Given my parents' harsh criticism of me, it's ridiculous for me never to be harsh with my own children." It's more rational for me to recognize when I'm being critical, admit it to myself and my children, and work on not being critical."

CHAPTER 9: SELF-KINDNESS

I am excited to tell you about self-kindness finally. Self-compassion begins with self-kindness. In some respects, all of this training has led us to the point where most former victims of childhood abuse will be ready, willing, and able to begin offering self-kindness to themselves. Unfortunately, as victims of childhood abuse, we must work extremely hard to think that we are deserving of self-kindness, let alone compassion from others. However, the good news is that you will not have to live the rest of your life without the capacity to treat yourself with care because of your efforts so far. You may begin right now.

In some respects, you've already started to learn to practice self-kindness. You can do it by putting an end to the constant self-judgment and self-criticism you've been used to. Understanding and accepting your flaws or faults rather than criticizing them is a crucial tactic.

What Does Kindness Feel Like?

The question that arises is, "what is self-kindness?" When you think about someone kind, what comes to your mind? What behaviors do you attribute to kindness?

Words of Kindness

1. Take some time to consider the phrases that come to mind when you think about compassion. Make a note of it on a piece of paper.

1. Now write how it feels to be the recipient of someone's warmth and compassion. What effect do you think it's having on your body?

I remember the first time someone was actually kind to me when I was nine years old. An elderly couple rented the house in front of ours. One of their older daughters flew down from Alaska to visit them. She was only with them for two weeks, but in that time, she changed my life. I'm not sure if she was nice to everyone, but she was really nice to me. She appeared to understand me better than most individuals I'd met. She made a point of coming out to meet me whenever she saw me in the yard or going home from school. She was curious about me and asked me questions about school and what I loved and disliked. On occasion, she would ask me inside for cupcakes and cookies. She made me feel as if someone genuinely cared about me and looked forward to seeing me for the brief time she was here.

She gave me a scarf with the phrase "Mexico" inscribed in huge glittering letters and an image of a bullfighter in a cape on the day she departed. It was fantastic. She assured me that I would be able to go to many other countries when I grew older. For years, I kept that scarf as a reminder of this lady's kindness and the fact that there were good people in the world. I also recalled her travel advice, and fantasizing about it helped me get through my miserable upbringing.

Who has been kind to you? Who treated you with interest and concern? Who made you feel like you mattered?

Remembering a Kind Person

1. Think back to a moment when you were a child or an adult, and someone was kind to you. Consider how this individual handled you. Did they talk to you in a caring manner or physically soothe you in any way?
2. Try to recall the expression on the person's face. What did this person's face say to you (acceptance, friendliness, generosity of spirit, for example)?
3. Try to recall what this individual said to you. Try to recall the person's voice or at least the message that their voice indicated to you.
4. Recall how it felt to be treated with compassion. What effect did it have on you? Allow yourself to immerse yourself in this feeling completely.
5. Describe how it felt to be treated with kindness, including how it made you feel in your body and how it made you think about yourself.

Defining Self-Kindness

1. Think about the kindest and most compassionate person you have ever known.
2. Try to find what made you feel so cared about.
3. Try to talk with yourself in the same way. Use the same words and tone.
4. Take a deep breath and slowly take in the feeling of love and kindness.

When I think of that lovely woman, the first thing that comes to me is how friendly she was every time she saw me. She constantly smiled and gave me the impression that she was delighted to see me. She spoke to me in a really compassionate manner, and she was quite attentive to me, asking me personal questions and genuinely listening to what I had to say. She demonstrated that she was paying attention to me by her face, nods, and comments. She also validated my sentiments, letting me know that it was natural for me to feel that way when I informed her.

So, when I chose to recreate my experience with her as a method of learning how to bring self-kindness to myself, I made sure to incorporate the following elements:

- When I was trying to make myself feel accepted and embraced for who I am, I started smiling at myself in the mirror as if to say "hi" and welcome myself.

- I was paying attention to myself and was curious about how I was feeling. Every day, I checked in with myself, asking how I was feeling (angry, sad, fearful, guilty, or ashamed?). Then I questioned myself why I was feeling this way and if I needed to do something about it. I rehearsed and attempted to speak to myself in a loving and welcoming manner.

- I started believing in myself. "It's normal that I feel this way," I told myself, validating my own sentiments.

Consider how you can imitate the conduct of a lovely individual you know. How can you start treating yourself right now? How did you want to be treated as a child?

A Word of Warning

You may encounter a situation in which you are bombarded with overwhelming sensations of sadness or other unpleasant emotions, as well as traumatic or painful memories, while you continue to practice self-kindness. As you incorporate self-kindness into your life, old basic ideas about yourself from infancy ("I'm unlovable"; "I'm useless") may surface from your subconscious.

This phenomenon was stated to me by a very caring therapist in the following way: When we initially begin working on our difficulties, we are like a vessel filled with feelings of humiliation, anguish, wrath, fear, and guilt. It's as if we're pouring love and compassion into that vessel as we begin to heal—especially when we begin to provide ourselves with self-compassion and self-kindness. We must make place for new good sensations of self-kindness and love because the vessel is full of shame and other negative emotions. Our guilt and other negative emotions begin to flood out in order to make place for feelings of self-kindness and love. As a result, the more sympathetic and kinder you are to yourself, the more pain for all the times you felt alone and misunderstood may surface.

The best method to cope with this expected circumstance is to confront it head-on rather than ignore negative emotions. "I've been feeling excellent about myself," you may remark. "It seems reasonable that past thoughts of self-doubt and self-hatred would resurface." Or, as you've been practicing, you may address your negative feelings by acknowledging that you're in pain and repeating any of the phrases you've been using to address and tend to your pain.

Don't be alarmed if deep sentiments such as sadness arise; simply let the feelings surface. Allow yourself to be sad for all the times you've been in agony with no one to console you. Simply said, try to be nice to yourself and relax from your suffering.

Making self-kindness a normal aspect of your life will require time and effort. You can, however, learn to listen to and respect your own needs. You can learn to pay attention to your body's cues instead of dismissing them. You also learn to love yourself even when you make errors by acquiring the ability to self-soothe.

Good news! There is a rewarding aspect to self-kindness. Every day provides you with a new opportunity to meet your suffering with kindness, and every time you do this, you deepen your belief that you deserve such kindness. The more graciously you respond to yourself when you make a mistake or when things go wrong, the more you will be able to undo the harm that years of self-criticism caused. The more you soothe and nourish yourself when you're unhappy, fearful, furious, or guilty, the less you'll be overwhelmed by your negative feelings.

Above all, remember that you deserve to be nice to yourself; you deserve to relax when you're anxious; and you deserve to understand and satisfy your fundamental human needs such as rest, adequate nourishment, and social interaction.

CHAPTER 10: SELF-ENCOURAGEMENT

This section is about how to develop self-encouragement to achieve your goals and dreams. This is valid for any goals you have set, whether to stop taking drugs or leave an abusive relationship.

The thing that limits your motivation is your inner critic voice. It undermines you and greatly demotivates you. The task is to get ahead of this and start your journey of self-encouragement.

How to Practice Self-Encouragement

Building oneself up rather than tearing yourself down is what self-encouragement entails. It's like being a loving parent to yourself, a mom who recognizes her child's potential and wants to foster it, a parent who is pleased with her child when he accomplishes his objectives. It is different than feeling envious or resentful because she never praised her child before. It is the process of believing in yourself and in your ability to overcome your limitations. Instead of focusing on your flaws and limits, self-encouragement focuses on your strengths, good characteristics, and skills. It entails ensuring that you're surrounded by individuals who will support you rather than criticize you—people who aren't scared by your success. It also entails concentrating on what you have done rather than what you haven't.

As you create your self-encouragement practice:

- Recognize where you could have ended up.
- Give yourself credit for what you've accomplished.
- Notice your positive and negative qualities and create a list accordingly.
- Be clear about what you want to accomplish.
- Replace self-criticism with self-correction.
- Be prepared for disappointments.
- Be prepared for your inner saboteur.

Talk to Your Inner Critic in a Compassionate Way

So, what should you do if you realize that you're having a significant negative reaction to positive changes? You may now use the compassionate self you've built instead of fighting your inner critic, as we described in previous chapters. You may use it to tell your inner critic that you don't have to act the way it wants you to—that your true self will take charge. Remind yourself that the criticism comes from a place of fear, grief, and past voices. You now feel more assertive, mature, and intelligent than your inner critic, and you can treat it with kindness instead of succumbing to the inner fear.

Compassion for Your Inner Critic

1. As you did before, sit in a comfortable posture and take many deep breaths. Bring your focus to your inner self or emotional regions.

2. You've been cultivating a compassionate self if you've been talking to yourself, nourishing yourself, and practicing self-kindness. If you're able, connect with your compassionate self right now. Feel your human strength, maturity, and wisdom.
3. Decide that you've reached a moment in your life where your compassionate self can take command.
4. Talk to your inner critic and remind yourself that the criticism comes from a place of fear and grief.
5. Allow your compassionate self to communicate with your inner critic now. Speak to him in a firm yet caring tone, letting your inner critic know that your compassionate self is now in command.

Some of the things my clients have spoken to their inner critics are as follows:

"I don't need it. I am capable of dealing with this."

"I'm sorry you're scared, furious, and vulnerable and that you're reacting badly as a result. But this isn't the way things should be.

"From now on, I'll be in command."

This method is particularly useful if you see your inner critic as a loving but mistaken father who only wants to protect you and keep you safe. Your actual parents may have been attempting to protect you, no matter how many bad messages they sent you (from disappointment, rejection, or failure). As a result, your inner critic was born to keep your parent close to you. But now, you don't need that inner critic, that withdrawn parent. Without all the negative signals and cautions, you now have a more compassionate self inside of you who will defend you in a better way.

CHAPTER 11: HOPE

To heal from trauma, pain, and loss is a very strenuous endeavor. Healing begins when a person admits that they are suffering from shame due to trauma and loss. Shame starts deep inside and grows, outwardly affecting behaviors, relationships, and one's general approach to life. Some attempt to bury these issues, believing that, if planted deep enough, the problems would not germinate and be visible. For others, shame comes out forcefully through rage, arrogance, and overbearingness. Still, some will become passive-aggressive, converting a response to the world in a co-dependent manner by working hard to meet the needs of others while simultaneously denying their own reality. Whatever the behavior is, the shame will inevitably present itself in one form or another. There is no denying it.

Acknowledging the root of your emotional pain, loss, trauma, hurt, shame, or disappointment may not be an easy process. One day, my client Eric sat in my office for therapy after recently leaving a relationship with his verbally and physically abusive wife. Eric had scars from the physical abuse that had required medical attention and stitches. Throughout the session, he would recount stories of the abuse he had endured with a smile on his face, sometimes even laughing about it. I noticed this unusual behavior quickly, realizing that Eric was clearly not identifying the pain he was experiencing. As time progressed, I learned that Eric's father died when he was only nine. Eric had personally seen his father crushed in a horrific bulldozing accident, adding great intensity to his loss. His mother was depressed after her husband's loss, as she was left to raise several children on her own, with Eric being the youngest. Eric committed to being as helpful as possible to his mother and never be a burden. Somewhere, within his mind as a child, he decided to keep a smile on his face and be a happy child that did not give his depressed mother anything else to worry about. Eric was living a lie, denying his own emotions and stuffing them further and further into the core of his existence.

Through therapy, I gently confronted Eric about the incongruent nature between his words and the emotions that such a story would typically evoke with the current feelings displayed on his face and through his body language. I often pointed out to him that he was smiling or giggling. The first few times, he acted surprised that I, as the therapist, reacted to his presentation. When he recounted these stories, I told him I was concerned for the little boy and the grown man carrying so much pain but wouldn't allow himself to experience it. After a few months of using the same intervention over and over, Eric started to identify with his own pain that was caused on that dreadful day when his life changed forever before his eyes. The layers of self-protection and preservation had to be peeled back so he could find his true emotional self. The process of admitting his deep pain took many therapy sessions and much remodeling to let him know it was okay for a "man" to experience his emotions and fully begin the healing process. I knew, when the emotional wall of self-preservation finally collapsed, there would be a great deal of emotional trauma for Eric to work through. Until that time arrived, Eric could not be helped through the stages of experiencing and facing his trauma.

CHAPTER 12: CLARITY

How can you make sense of the trauma that you have endured and its result in stigma? Once a person acknowledges the trauma and stigma, the next step is to find clarity. The process of looking at the scenario objectively while also recognizing the subjective experience is "clarity." You have always lived your life from a subjective point of view — noticing how you personally experienced it, how you felt, and the shame within you due to childhood abuse. Your reality is your perception. How you experience something shapes your thoughts, feelings, and beliefs about the event, yourself, and your environment. Over time your perception becomes your truth. The clarification comes from recognizing that there is another reality besides the one in which you personally live. The reality of the situation may be different from your perception of it.

The same was the case with Jenson. He always assumed that his father didn't like him and wanted nothing to do with him. Still, as he later discovered, his father's avoidance of interaction was his way of protecting him and allowing Jenson to be a kid, free from child abuse. Once Jenson received clarification regarding the facts of the event, he could see the situation more objectively and begin processing it on a level not available to him before this understanding.

Clarity now and again comes from extremely sudden and unexpected situations. Jenson was not hoping to get any information about his father's past on the day he was comfortable sharing his story. He was not expecting to discover that his dad really adored him and protected him from the start. Here and there, scenarios will change your perception of your trauma, yet the shame can regularly continue. The death of an individual or the confession of a secret can alter your subjective perception.

At other times there will be no circumstances to give clarity. You may just realize you don't care how you feel, don't feel like yourself, and don't care for the unfortunate and unhealthy patterns you keep on repeating. Clarity might need to come through professional mediation and intervention from a professional. It frequently takes handling life circumstances by a professional to see that there is one more reality other than the one you are living. Now and again, having someone else pay attention and listen can help you navigate and find clarity. Over the long haul, the waters of your thoughts have become so muddied with your encounters with disgrace, self-hatred, shame, and agony that you can't see clearly, or objectively. Your future way might seem impassible, without a clear heading for gaining positive progress.

How do you find someone to help discover clarity? Locating a trusted and competent therapist can sometimes be a difficult process. There is a long list of therapists and trained professionals in the phone book or online, but that does not mean that they are quality therapists with a background in trauma recovery. It is important to do adequate research before selecting a therapist. Ask questions about a prospective therapist's specializations to help you make an informed decision about which therapist is a good fit for you.

The therapeutic relationship set up between a trained professional and a client is of principal and paramount significance. Many counseling and advising course books will refer to explore therapy options that aren't really the kind of treatment you are looking for and that works with healing. The thing that will be of paramount help is the strength of the specialist/patient relationship. Discovering a specialist you interface with and trust is an unquestionable and essential requirement. You will share your inner and most intimate feelings with this professional. You must build up trust with this professional and have a sense of security, and you must feel genuinely acknowledged. Most people won't stay in treatment and fail to heal if this relationship is not fully there. If you are in a therapeutic relationship and don't feel the aura of trust and security, or don't feel it is useful — move on! Discover somebody who provides you with a feeling of inside harmony, peace, trust, and wellbeing.

Even though the therapeutic relationship is the foundation of successful therapy, I think the therapist needs to have the explicit specializations you might desire. Always try to look for a therapist who has relevant experience and knows various techniques for treating trauma. This is why you needed this book, as I have the knowledge as well as the personal experience with childhood abuse.

I hear you when you say it is not easy to cope with such painful memories.

Also, there is a wide range of therapies in the area of brain science and counseling. Most insurance agencies attempt to mandate the utilization of a fairly fast and short-term therapy known as Cognitive-Behavioral Therapy (CBT). Normally, insurance agencies consider it to be cost-effective. It doesn't mean that it's not a powerful choice for the patient. The reason for CBT is that one's irrational thoughts and feelings are causing situational interpretations and understandings, which lead to deceptions and false beliefs, bringing about misled social behavior and reactions. Even though there is accuracy to these assumptions, I trust CBT is simply viable to treat certain cases or entirely successful to some extent, as for treating different phobias and fears. It tends to be useful to inspect and examine the flawed beliefs and comprehensions about oneself or the assumptions of gender and gender roles. If CBT is utilized with a trauma patient, I don't really accept and believe it to be a beneficial therapy. It is ideal whenever combined with other, more successful types of treatment. An individual encountering trauma and shame have further issues to determine past cognitive distortions. I urge people to look for professionals trained in psychodynamic hypotheses and theories, Internal Family Systems, and other Interpersonal type therapies.

New patients frequently tell me that they have no interest in delving into their past and only want to resolve their current problems. I always interpret this in one of two ways: either the patient is not fully educated about the purpose of therapy, or the patient is not yet ready for the rigorous process of effective therapy work. Though some need help working through a current, specific problem, most people are truly an amalgamation of their experiences. Experiences shape us and become our reality, guiding our present behavior. How can you solve a present problem without fully examining how your current belief system was formed? If the issue you are going through is a repeated pattern, deeper work needs to be done. An examination of your past will most likely help uncover important information and promote a healthy change.

Freud and other early psychoanalytic theorists may have taken more of a parental blame approach. However, effective therapy is not about finding or placing blame, whether it is from past experiences with parents or other prominent figures in one's life. Therapy is a journey of walking through your experiences to glean understanding from your past life events. It is concerned with looking at the subjective and becoming objective; it helps you examine the factual. Remember the five areas of a child's healthy development as proposed by Pia Melody: Value, Vulnerable, Imperfect, Dependent, and Spontaneous.

Therapy examines the experience of each of these concepts. Trauma may have occurred not because of events but perhaps what wasn't included as part of the developmental phase. For example, one of my client's father's lack of involvement in each area profoundly affected his son's gender role conflict and gender identity development. Therapy is often an examination of where your development may have gone awry due to abuse, neglect, specific traumas, and the experience of shame. It is typically about the process, not the "who" that caused changes to a belief system. Often, significant life players will be discussed, and there can be specific individuals at the source of pain and trauma, but healing does not come through the placement of blame. Healing comes through objective clarity — releasing the binding shame and resolving the necessary steps through therapy interventions.

Many therapists will ask new clients what their goals are for therapy. This may be the therapist's attempt to identify expectations, receive insight into a client's issues, and determine where they may already be within the stages of healing. Before entering therapy, it is helpful, though not necessary, for patients to consider their expectations and how these translate into personal goals. Though helpful, clients often cannot express specific goals, but only problem identification: they can communicate the problem and identify a behavioral pattern they want to change. Finding clarity about what you need from counseling may be part of your therapy process. It is not a requirement to enter treatment with goals in place.

CHAPTER 13: HEALING

The recovering phase of therapy, otherwise known as the "working through" phase of therapy, is the place where the genuine work happens. When patients with a previous history of childhood abuse arrive at this point, they ought to have set up a trusting, caring therapeutic relationship. It is an ideal opportunity to dive into the individual's story. In the therapeutic system, the professionals help the abused person in fact-examination and feeling-identification. It helps them develop an intelligible entire from these pieces permitting objective understanding. This approach supports testing their thoughts and subjectivity; and assists the client with figuring out the thing which is valuable and which can be disposed of.

For some, the trauma and shame have stayed a secret. It is a force lying deep inside and is frequently very much guarded. Many individuals have worked for quite a long time to keep these parts from truly being seen by another person; just the pad on their bed knows about the tears and the assault they have faced. I used to say, "You are just pretty much as wiped out as your mysteries." Our secrets develop inside us, regularly progressively misshaping our existence and reality. For some, who start therapy, they at first can't comprehend telling someone else their abstract insight.

Discovering the mental fortitude to recount your story and to open your secrets to someone else is amazing and powerful. It might be hard at first. However, secrets lead to detachment and shame that will bind oneself. You have the right to be free — you have the right to heal. Accepting that you have the right to heal is one more fundamental stage toward healing. A therapy room isn't a court, and judgment has no spot there. Rather, therapy is a place where you feel safe to share your story. As a therapist, my job is to assist individuals in telling their stories, allowing them to release their secrets and eliminate their shame.

Through vulnerability, one concedes and perceives the shame, shares it with another, and can make the essential strides towards genuine recovery and healing. Your sharing demonstration can be in a therapy room, a self-help gathering, with your support partner, or in group therapy. Regardless of the setting, it is basic to discover the fortitude to become vulnerable and comfortable with yourself.

Sharing activates the process of healing emotionally, physically, and on a neurophysiological and neurobiological level. The client's willingness and ability to share their story is of greatest concern to their therapist. In my therapeutic practice, I must create a safe, caring environment where the client can risk vulnerability: telling their story and letting their secrets be made known so they can ultimately advance toward healing.

When in the midst of simply sharing your story, it is common to have sudden moments of clarity and insight. Insight is gaining awareness of new knowledge and identifying a deep, intuitive understanding of yourself, your thoughts and feelings, your behavior, or some combination thereof. These moments of insight are like turning on a light inside of a dark, musty cellar only to find unrealized valuables. Insight is the catalyst that fosters change.

Insight can be fostered in many ways, especially through therapy sessions. It is not uncommon for issues to be intergenerational, and because of this, I often conduct a family genogram, going back at least three generations. A genogram can quickly illuminate patterns within a family system. To do this, clients supply the name and age of their ancestors, mark if they are dead or living, and give a full description of each individual's personality. They share the memories that stand out most about this person, any addictive behaviors that are known, and any form of abuse the person endured or afflicted. Once the genogram is completed, it is easier to recognize familial patterns. For example, a great-grandfather may have abandoned his young children after having an affair. The grandfather followed the same pattern, the client's father did as well, and now the young male client sits in my office, hoping not to repeat the same destructive patterns of his forefathers.

The next tool for building insight is often a life timeline. Clients examine their life by beginning with early development to identify the attachment types they experienced with their caregivers. As the timeline progresses, I ask the individual to identify significant memories and events, memories of abuse and/or neglect, sexual development, relationships, hurts, and triumphs. Again, this process typically fosters great insight. It also provides me, as the therapist, an opportunity to draw conclusions and test hypotheses based on the collaborative work of the genogram and the timeline.

Many questions are posed throughout the therapeutic process, and patients need to examine where boundary violations have occurred and the response to these significant events. We have three modes of responding in the face of trauma: fight, flight, or freeze. I pose questions like these to my patients:

- How did you respond?
- What was the experience like?
- What are you continuing to experience as a result of your response?
- Where do you feel this in your body?

Not all important insights and points of understanding happen inside the therapy room. Having clients read books as an ancillary to therapy can assist in the recovery time and degree of healing a person can experience. I believe that the more a person can make sense and meaning of their experience, the greater the healing. Therefore, I often suggest to individuals that it will help to read books related to their situation.

As a therapist, I look for patterns, especially if situations develop from attachment issues or trauma early in life. I attempt to take the pieces of a person's story and put the puzzle together, creating a unique mosaic of their life. I then can help my patients put these pieces together with insight, understanding, and meaning. With the objective help of a therapist, one can begin seeing other realities instead of the one they have lived. They are now more equipped to see their own life objectively, making sense of their experience and behavior. Insight can be powerful to the change process.

Throughout therapy, I am acutely listening for the presence of shame and where it affects the individual. I listen closely to experienced traumas, and specifically, how these traumas bred shame. Because shame is an internal type of mental scrutiny, it leads to self-disparaging behaviors. If this process is reoccurring, the shame becomes toxic shame. Similarly, if abuse occurs repeatedly, it often leads to complex trauma. As a therapist, my role is to help patients understand how toxic shame and complex trauma work together to destroy the self through unhealthy thoughts, feeling, and behavior patterns.

CHAPTER 14: CHANGE

Change can happen! You are ready for change when you have unpacked your personal baggage and swiped through the contents, making sense of its meaning. Change begins by learning how to accept yourself for who you are —flaws, gifts, talents, and all. Once we have acknowledged all the aspects of who we are, we can learn to accept the self and all the unique positive and negative characteristics that make up our whole. We all have a story; we all have hurts and pains from the past; we all possess the power of choice, not always making good decisions for ourselves; and we all have character flaws. A person in the change stage is learning to accept themselves with their strengths and weaknesses. This involves re-thinking and re-working your self-concept, beginning with self-acceptance and self-esteem.

Self-acceptance and self-esteem are not the same concepts. Self-esteem refers to the positive feelings we have about the parts of ourselves that we see as good. Self-acceptance, however, is much broader. We unconditionally approach self-acceptance, accepting ourselves globally, including both our strengths and weaknesses. We see ourselves as a work in progress through self-acceptance and accept that some parts are better developed than others. It allows us to recognize and acknowledge our hurts, habits, and hang-ups, as well as our strengths.

The basis for the self-acceptance process comes from witnessing the ability of our primary caregivers to accept us, allowing us to have value, vulnerability, imperfection, dependence, and to be spontaneous without shame. In early childhood, we do not possess the ability to see ourselves separately from our parents. As we progress through the maturation process, we gain a sense of self. How a caregiver has modeled and demonstrated self-acceptance is our first introduction to the process. If, through this process, there were conditions of 'earning' worth, learning to accept oneself may be a life-long challenge fully. Parents and primary caregivers provide us with a model of caring and parenting that later becomes our own self-care and self-parenting.

Although therapy is not about finding and placing blame, at times, those who have abused us must be identified and confronted. If an individual has experienced abuse, neglect, bullying, and other harmful treatments, a confrontation may be warranted; however, it must be done constructively for closure and healing. One must carefully examine who and how to confront. A verbal or physical attack on someone who has hurt you will not bring closure. Confrontation must be planned out and timed accordingly. A therapist can help you identify if it is appropriate to confront the person and the likelihood of any resulting harm or further damage.

A confrontation is not intended to get revenge. The patient should carefully work with a therapist to identify their goals for the confrontation: it is typically used as an intervention to help resolve and bring closure to past trauma. If confronting a person has the potential of re-traumatizing the individual, the therapist should discourage the event. Confrontations must be planned to help resolve unfinished issues and return the shame to the person it belongs to. One cannot initiate a confrontation hoping to hear specific words or see specific behaviors from the antagonist; often, they will not give you what you want. One cannot anticipate an admission of wrongdoing or an apology. A confrontation is used to allow an individual who has been hurt to find their voice, share their secret, speak their truth, acknowledge what has happened, and give the shame back to the source so the patient can let go of the carried, toxic shame.

Some individuals will feel the need to forgive the person who wronged them to let go of the anger and shame they have carried. If forgiveness is possible, it is encouraged; however, it is important to remember that forgiveness does not mean reconciliation. Forgiveness does not require entering back into a relationship with the person who hurt them. Often, revitalizing such a relationship would be an unhealthy choice. Part of the confrontation is re-establishing boundaries with this person, and sometimes those boundaries include severing contact with them.

Another step in the change process is deciding if you had any responsibility for the events that transpired. Please note that any physical, sexual, verbal, or neglect abuse is never a child's fault — they are never to blame for their own abuse. It is the adult's responsibility to protect them. At times, individuals will blame themselves for abuse, especially in cases of sexual abuse.

In some cases, an individual may determine they did have some responsibility for the event or even have replicated the hurt done to them. Sometimes, to gain control over feelings of loss and abandonment, individuals will repeat the pattern of abuse that they endured. Psychodynamic theory has termed this as "identification with the aggressor." Instead of facing the hurt and loss of control one might feel from abusive events, a person will identify with their aggressor and traumatize others to regain the feeling of power and control initially taken from them. These individuals need to own their behavior and the hurt that they have caused to others. Self-examination to determine the degree of your responsibility is an important part of the healing process.

When making amends with a person is impossible, there are many other symbolic ways to resolve and forgive one's behavior. For instance, a therapist may ask the individual to write letters of responsibility and read them aloud during their session to help process the associated feelings. If you have the opportunity to be in group therapy, the therapist may ask you to pick out another group member to represent the other person while you read your letter or process the event. Whatever therapeutic method is chosen, the individual must find a path to self-forgiveness. The freedom that comes through this process can be the impetus for change.

Mindfulness

Many of us go through life on automatic pilot. Every day, we exist as if we were robots, with no regard for the options available to us. We let our old patterns control what we do and think. We've been walking down the same well-worn route for so long that we've come to believe this is what life is all about. We naively accept it and refuse to think that it can be improved or changed. We might become so engrossed in the old patterns that we fail to notice that we are merely surviving rather than living.

As you pay attention to yourself and focus on your time, you may see patterns of negative ideas entering your inner world. Our irrational negative thinking has a direct impact on our ability to cope with pain and suffering. We reinforce our negative sentiments when we indulge in harmful thoughts, which erode our self-esteem. These ideas aren't new. They didn't happen because you ended your abusive relationship. They changed with time and over the course of your life. It's possible that you're just noticing them now since you've turned off your autopilot.

We typically imagine that hundreds, if not thousands, of thoughts are running through our heads at the same time.

In reality, we can only have one single notion in our heads at any given time. The continual flood of thoughts, views, and beliefs bombarding our awareness are all competing for the same mental place in our awareness.

Simply put, if you're thinking about your upcoming exciting adventure with buddies, that's the only thing on your mind. This is the thought that is occupying your lonely cognitive region if you are worried about how your abuser was a genuinely disgusting scoundrel. We might become confused because our thoughts move from one concept to the next at breakneck speed, but only one idea can take center stage in our consciousness at any given time.

We may use it by consciously shifting our single thought away from a detrimental intrusive idea and toward something else. This may be accomplished by paying attention to our internal environment, including our thoughts, feelings, and bodily sensations, and making a deliberate decision about how to respond to them at any particular time. "Mindfulness" refers to the act of increasing our consciousness and paying attention to what is going on inside us.

Mindfulness, by default, puts us into the present moment. It causes us to draw our attention back to what is going on in the here and now. This simple change can transform you from the inside out.

We are responsible for what goes on in our inner world, just as we are responsible for our happiness. You may not know what it feels like to be happy and whole inside your own skin at this time in your life. You may find yourself in a chronic state of fear, "doing" instead of "being." When we are being, we are not running around taking care of chores or trying to solve the mysteries of the universe. We are one with ourselves, wholly, and at the same time, relaxed. When we are being, we just are. We are right here, right now, not in the past and not in the future.

Being is not procrastination. Weird as this may sound, being is doing. You are allowing things to move and transform into a new state, a state where the ego is released, and you no longer have to use your energy to propel you forward or hold you back. A mental notion, a belief, or an expectation does not form the basis of your life. When you are being, you are going with the flow of the universe and not pushing your agenda forward, whatever it may be.

This state of existence may feel uncomfortable. You may be accustomed to knowing what your next step will be or having your life planned out months in advance. It is reasonable not to know. When we are being, we have taken a step back from the working of the brain. We have opened ourselves up to the guidance that our soul provides. When we are being, we recognize that we are not in charge, and we cannot control the outcome of any given situation. We are allowing the energy of the universe to travel through us uninhibited. This free flow of energy permits our lives to unravel on their own terms.

From this place of objectivity, we can see that resistance is not the way to go, but at the same time, we may find that investing more time and energy (unless prompted) into our affairs is not right either. We discover that the best way of dealing with any situation is to let go of any presupposed notion of how it should be and allow it to unfold before us. Any decisions we may have to make, in turn, will seem harmonious to us, regardless of how hard they may appear.

Sometimes when we are in this place, we are led to do things that can, to the rational mind, seem like a complete mystery. We may find that we are guided to faraway places or are compelled to open the door to possibilities we may never have imagined before. At other times we might unknowingly put ourselves into situations that on the surface may seem traumatic, painful, or at odds with ourselves, but as time passes, we will often look back at these moments and recognize their perfection. Regardless of what it is, we work to accept what life hands us with open arms.

This state of peace is what "being" instead of doing or reacting feels like. There is a sense of inner calmness that words cannot adequately describe. People who feel emotionally safe tend to do better when trying to find this place within themselves. They are not battling with intrusive thoughts or raging emotions. Mindfulness can be used to help you feel this way regularly. Wouldn't that be wonderful!

Mindfulness Practice

If the peace and serenity of beingness is the goal, where are you now? We all have moments when life events disturb our inner world.

Depending on what it is, we may be able to quickly recover our composure and return to our normal healthy and happy state. At other times, situations can set something off within which we may find challenging, if not impossible, to shake off. If you think about it, when you are caught up in a cycle of worry or rumination, you are bogged down, living with an inner world filled with pain, shame, self-criticism, or judgment. You are not happy. You are hurting.

When you feel anxious, upset, hurt, or frustrated, there is a disruption in the force. One of your inner wounds, a previous trauma, or a negative core belief may have become activated. There may be a conflict between what your authentic self wants and the precepts stored in your unconscious mind. You may still try to fit into the square box society, or your early programming has been erected. It may also indicate that you are in an abusive or toxic situation, especially if you consistently find yourself being negatively affected at the hand or the mouth of another.

Any of these things can cause a disturbance within you. You may find yourself, when this occurs, reactively responding to the situation using a primitive defense mechanism or caught up in a cycle of negative thought. We cannot use these moments to become our own private detective and solve the mystery of what is happening.

Identifying what set you off can be challenging to determine. You can, nevertheless, ready the stage for profound healing by getting to know what elicits your negative responses. These insights might help you learn how to react to scenarios that once distressed you with more mature coping mechanisms.

When you begin the practice of mindfulness, you will quickly discover that you are not your thoughts. You are not your fears and not your insecurities. You will start to notice that it is just energy, an emotion, stimulated in you. We never respond to something emotionally unless there is a conscious or unconscious thought tied to it. From this position, you can begin to observe your thoughts and embark on connecting the dots between them and your emotional responses. It is okay to be with your thoughts and experience your emotional state. You can do it without reacting to them or judging them. It is easier than it may initially sound.

We reinforce our unwanted or intrusive thoughts the more we think about them. They can become trapped in our one empty mental slot and arouse similar negative thoughts and emotions. It can be like the ball in a pinball machine. Our negative thinking can begin bouncing off the bumpers of our other false beliefs and inner wounds until our insides are shouting.

You can start the process of calming down what has flared up and hopefully let go of the rest by being mindful of your thoughts, especially your intrusive ones. They can be easier to control and can even be prevented if you catch them early instead of waiting until you are in the midst of a full-blown meltdown.

Mindful meditation

One way of supporting our ability to "be" is through meditation. Some people suggest that self-improvement techniques such as meditation or mindfulness are hard or even exhausting. The underlying stress and a pattern of negative thoughts are even more taxing on your body and soul.

Numerous meditation rehearses use mindfulness as their fundamental foundations. When we consider meditation in the west, we imagine an Indian spiritualist wearing a beautiful robe sitting in a lotus position on the highest point of a mountain. We might take long to encounter the ecstatic states detailed by these blessed men. However, we may think that it is specifically difficult to accomplish. This impression of meditation makes many shy in any event. It makes them not even start or give up easily on this.

The main objective of meditation, like mindfulness, is to center our focus and our thoughts on a single agenda. When we immerse ourselves in one task or one thought pattern, we end up losing track of everything else around us. Controlling what the mind focuses on allows any intrusive thoughts that may be vying for our attention to slip gently away. This practice helps to calm the soul and supports our body as it discharges harmful energy and emotions.

What many of us don't understand is that two unique kinds of mindful meditation can be utilized. The main sort of meditation is called passive meditation. This unwinding and relaxing method is the thing that we frequently imagine when we attempt to meditate.

Passive meditation fuses techniques like rehashing a mantra or insistence, zeroing in on our breath, or clearing the mind of thought. It isn't the breath, the mantra, or even the demonstration of keeping the brain clear that supports healing. At the point when we center our brains around something, anything, it fills our unfilled opening. It has the additional advantage of disconnecting us from the occasionally wild elements and dynamics going on inside. We find ourselves in a tangled up web of ever-changing thoughts. That is why they call mindfulness and meditation "a practice." It can take us a while to retrain our brains and begin to form new neural pathways that support mental calmness.

The second kind of meditation is active meditation. You have presumably already experienced active meditation in your life and didn't have any acquaintance with it. Think when you were wound up agitated, diverted, or feeling ungrounded. Perhaps in the middle of your traumatic experience with past abuse, you went to the fitness center and had an intense exercise. Your session closes, and as you leave the fitness center, you find that you feel quiet, clear, and strikingly stimulated. Indeed, exercising can be a type of active meditation. The same is valid for jogging, running, raking leaves, cleaning a bath, or playing out a custom.

What matters is the intensity you employ as you pursue any of these activities. Your mind focuses on one thing and one thing only. You can practice mindful meditation anytime and anywhere. You can do it while you are brushing your teeth or washing the dishes, going for a walk, or reading a book. It is about keeping your attention on what is going on at that particular moment. Gently bring your mind back to the original focal point if you find it wandering. Be kind to yourself as you begin doing this. With a little time and practice, you will see immense changes occurring right before your eyes.

CHAPTER 15: GETTING CLEAR

First and essential on the rundown list is, you need to know what you really need. You need an unmistakable and clear image of it. At this point, you ought to have clear comprehension and understanding of what your identity is and what you need in your relationships. In case you are uncertain, maybe making a list of every one of the potential outcomes and possibilities will assist you with narrowing down your idea, thoughts, and sentiments.

For example, do you want your abuser to stay at a distance when complete separation is not possible? Do they need to be alone when having an emotional breakdown? Do you want to be with someone kind, loving, and affectionate, attentive to you and your needs, articulate, and emotionally mature?

These are only a few things you can contemplate as you identify your relationship needs with the abuser. It is better to keep your requests general in nature.

Also, try not to fill your list with negatives. Identifying the fact that you do not want to be with a slob will only work to defeat your purpose. The universe will not hear, "I do not want to be with a slob," but only "Slob." Rephrase your inventory from what you do not want to what you do. This list will also support you down the road once you start meeting people to help you weed out who you might want to keep from those you want to toss back.

Become mindful of any negative thought patterns that may arise as you do this. Remember, negative thinking only sabotages your ability to have what you truly desire. Breathe, ground, and focus if need be. Trust that the universe has your best interests at heart. Trust dissolves fears. You cannot be afraid if you trust.

See it, feel it, experience it as if it were real. Imagine it in your mind's eye. Allow your desires to become emotionally charged. Believe in yourself and your future. Set your intentions. Feelings are the driving force behind the Law of Attraction. Our emotional energy activates our mental images and puts them in motion. They are then transmitted out into the universe via our energy systems. Be patient while you await its reply.

Taking Action

Making a move or taking action is a basic step in making your dreams work out as you expected. By moving toward accomplishing your objectives, you will set the Natural Laws of the Universe into movement. Steps, regardless of their size, oil the gears of the universe and permit it to work in the manner it is intended to work.

Numerous people accept they should simply make a vision board (a realistic portrayal, which can be utilized to assist with explaining your goals), rehash assertions, or keep up with positive thoughts. Without action, nothing can be accomplished. Assuming you need another relationship, trusting, wishing, and asking about it will do nothing but bad if you don't put yourself out there to meet new admirers.

Gratitude

The last piece, when working with your behavioral changes, is appreciation and gratitude. Say thank you for the favors you get. By perceiving and recognizing even the littlest things you are getting in your life, you can start to get greater and better things. Ideally, that will help you find the inner peace you have been searching for since the abuse happened.

At last, the recovery from trauma isn't tied to getting another vehicle, a huge pile of cash, distinction, or fortunes. It is tied to keeping ourselves in arrangement with the flow of life, permitting it and not our inner self to lead the way. This way, we open ourselves up to the beauty of nature and bring to ourselves those things we want.

I wish you a life full of blessings and prosperity.

CONCLUSION

Childhood abuse takes a toll on one's personal, social and emotional health. It is not your fault that a person abused you at a very fragile age when you could not face the trauma. It doesn't mean that you are spoiled or less than any other individual on planet earth. You have all the right to live a happy life full of dignity and compassion. This is not the end but the beginning of the changes you can create in your life by practicing self-compassion. You will find that the more compassionate you are toward yourself, the more you will feel compelled to take better care of yourself and surround yourself with people who respect you and treat you well. Slowly you will notice that you compare yourself to other people less often. You will find that you can evaluate yourself not on your performance, your looks, or the amount of money you make but by how well you are doing at taking care of your needs and providing yourself with the things you missed out on as a child. You will feel like you "fit in" more with other people and will have less of a need to isolate yourself from others.

Once you no longer have to work as hard to defend against your shame, you will be able to take your blinders off and actually see other people's pain and suffering—including the pain and suffering you may have caused. For those of you who have become abusive, this means you will be far less likely to re-offend. Once much of your stigma and pain has been eliminated, you can afford to face yourself much more honestly, including admitting when you have been abusive in the past and catching yourself when you start to become abusive in the present.

Resources

[1] Germer, C. K., & Neff, K. D. (2015). Cultivating self-compassion in trauma survivors. *Mindfulness-oriented interventions for trauma: Integrating contemplative practices*, 43-58.

[1] Keene, A. C., & Epps, J. (2016). Childhood physical abuse and aggression: Shame and narcissistic vulnerability. *Child Abuse & Neglect, 51*, 276-283.

[1] Middelton-Moz, J. (2020). *Shame & guilt: Masters of disguise*. Simon and Schuster.

[1] Robertson, T. E., Sznycer, D., Delton, A. W., Tooby, J., & Cosmides, L. (2018). The true trigger of shame: Social devaluation is sufficient, wrongdoing is unnecessary. *Evolution and Human Behavior, 39*(5), 566-573.

[1] Irons, C., & Lad, S. (2017). Using compassion focused therapy to work with shame and self-criticism in complex trauma. *Australian Clinical Psychologist, 3*(1), 1743.

[1] Braehler, C., & Neff, K. (2020). Self-compassion in PTSD. In *Emotion in posttraumatic stress disorder* (pp. 567-596). Academic Press.

[1] Kuo, J. R., Khoury, J. E., Metcalfe, R., Fitzpatrick, S., & Goodwill, A. (2015). An examination of the relationship between childhood emotional abuse and borderline personality disorder features: The role of difficulties with emotion regulation. *Child abuse & neglect, 39*, 147-155.

[1] Witbrodt, J., Kaskutas, L. A., & Grella, C. E. (2015). How do recovery definitions distinguish recovering individuals? Five typologies. *Drug and alcohol dependence, 148*, 109-117.

[1] Barlow, M. R., Turow, R. E. G., & Gerhart, J. (2017). Trauma appraisals, emotion regulation difficulties, and self-compassion predict posttraumatic stress symptoms following childhood abuse. *Child abuse & neglect*, *65*, 37-47.

[1] Kessler, R. C., Aguilar-Gaxiola, S., Alonso, J., Benjet, C., Bromet, E. J., Cardoso, G., ... & Koenen, K. C. (2017). Trauma and PTSD in the WHO world mental health surveys. *European journal of psychotraumatology*, *8*(sup5), 1353383.

[1] McConnico, N., Boynton-Jarrett, R., Bailey, C., & Nandi, M. (2016). A framework for trauma-sensitive schools. *Zero to Three*, *36*(5), 36-44.

[1] Woodyatt, L., Wenzel, M., & Griffin, B. J. (Eds.). (2017). *Handbook of the psychology of self-forgiveness* (pp. 2-28). Springer International Publishing.

[1] Kivity, Y., Tamir, M., & Huppert, J. D. (2016). Self-acceptance of negative emotions: the positive relationship with effective cognitive reappraisal. *International Journal of Cognitive Therapy*, *9*(4), 279-294.

[1] Salimi Bajestani, H. (2015). The Effectiveness of Self-Encouragement Training in Mental Health of Women with Addicted Spouses. *Scientific Quarterly Research on Addiction*, *9*(34), 67-78.

[1] Sege, R. D., & Browne, C. H. (2017). Responding to ACEs with HOPE: health outcomes from positive experiences. *Academic pediatrics*, *17*(7), S79-S85.

[1] Evans, G. J., Reid, G., Preston, P., Palmier-Claus, J., & Sellwood, W. (2015). Trauma and psychosis: The mediating role of self-concept clarity and dissociation. *Psychiatry Research*, *228*(3), 626-632.

[1] Jeong, S., & Cha, C. (2019). Healing from childhood sexual abuse: A meta-synthesis of qualitative studies. *Journal of child sexual abuse*, *28*(4), 383-399.

[1] Renna, M. E., Peng, J., Shrout, M. R., Madison, A. A., Andridge, R., Alfano, C. M., ... & Kiecolt-Glaser, J. K. (2021). Childhood abuse histories predict steeper inflammatory trajectories across time. *Brain, behavior, and immunity*, *91*, 541-545.

Made in the USA
Coppell, TX
01 October 2023